Haunted
Homeplace

Tales from the Borderlands of Tennessee & Kentucky

Beverly Forehand

ISBN 978-1-9393060-1-2

Library of Congress Catalog Number: 2014950657

First Edition

Printed in the United States of America
Published by 23 House Publishing
SAN 299-8084
www.23house.com

For Sarah, who isn't afraid of the dark.

Table of Contents

"From ghoulies and ghosties
And long-leggedy beasties
And things that go bump in the night,
Good Lord, deliver us!"
— Traditional Scottish prayer

"Then away out in the woods I heard that kind of a sound that a ghost makes when it wants to tell about something that's on its mind and can't make itself understood, and so can't rest easy in its grave, and has to go about that way every night grieving."

Mark Twain, *The Adventures of Huckleberry Finn*

On Stories

Stories are living things. They want to be told. It's the way they grow. Each time you share a story, it changes a bit. It becomes a part of the storyteller and the listener. A good story may stick with you for a lifetime, and a good ghost story never stops haunting you.

I've collected stories all my life and in my line of work I've been lucky enough to meet many people with a passion for a tale well told. There is, after all, no greater pleasure that sitting in front of a fire, with a warm mug listening to someone tell a story that chills you to the bone. Those are the stories you remember. Those are the stories that you pass on.

I hope you enjoy these stories. Most are about ghosts, some are about the supernatural, and all are about the South. Take them, make them yours, pass them along, and maybe I'll hear them again sometime, slightly different, but always the same, around a campfire.

Chapter 1:
Homeplace

As a child, my cousins and I saw plenty of ghosts at my grandmother's house, situated as it was beside a family cemetery. Only a couple of us would still admit to having seen them although we all believed at the time. Any eight-year-old, at night, in a dark room overlooking a graveyard will believe what he or she sees. But a twenty-year-old with twelve years behind him and only a memory for a guide will usually say how silly it was to think the neighbor's pale dog was a ghost. It must've been a tree or a shadow or a person taking a midnight walk, right? There's no way it was a ghost. There are more than years between childhood and adulthood.

That's not to say that adults don't believe in spirits. Some no doubt do. But nearly all children have a wholehearted belief. Even when their parents tell them there aren't ghosts or that there's nothing in the closet, they don't really believe it. Kids know that parents, however well-meaning, are often wrong. After all, how can a parent's logic stand up to the gut feeling of an eight-year-old? There are things in the dark that you can only see when you truly believe.

When my sister and I were children, we spent a lot of time at my grandmother's house which was conveniently right across the road. We lived in the country where there are no streetlights, no noises other than owls and cows after midnight, and you can really see the stars. Sometimes we would sleep out in my Granny's back yard in cub-tents with my faithful dog, Samson, at our feet. Sometimes we slept in a pile of cousins in the big main room with the fireplace and Grandfather clock. It didn't seem to matter where we slept. We usually saw something. Once we saw a patch of white mist rise up out of the graveyard and move slowly down the road. Once we saw a

3

pale face looking in the bedroom window. He tapped on the window once and smiled and then faded away. Sometimes appliances would turn themselves on and off again without being plugged in. Often we saw a small blue-white light on the back porch circling and bobbing for hours.

Our parents told us that we'd eaten too much sugar, stayed up too late, excited ourselves with nonsense, or watched too many scary movies. But my grandmother told us they were ghosts. She wasn't alarmed. She said it matter-of-factly. We lived by the family cemetery and, apparently, family members, alive or dead, were to be accorded visiting privileges. My grandmother visited the graveyard often and brought flowers cut from her garden or plants for the graves. She talked to the people buried there. She'd tell them what was going on with the family. I suppose she believed it only right that they should visit her as well.

My grandmother's ghosts never caused any problems. They were in the house, the barn, the yard, and the graveyard. They sometimes made noises, but never anything loud—quiet shuffling, tapping, a rush of wind. My Granny said you could talk to them if you had a mind to. She talked to them. I never did. I didn't really know what to say. I was always a little afraid of them—just like I was nervous around relatives I didn't know at the family reunion.

Since my grandmother has died, her house is closed up. It's a farmhouse over two hundred years old. For the first time in two centuries, no one lights a fire in the fireplace, no one cooks dinner in the kitchen, no one sleeps in the back bedroom on the wrought iron bed. I often wonder if the ghosts still visit. Are they disappointed that there's no one to see? Do they miss my grandmother's visits to their graves? Or do they talk to her in person now? Somehow, I think that it wasn't the house that they came to see, but my grandmother herself. Certainly, she saw ghosts in places other than her home. She saw them at my Aunt's house, in the fields, and on the road. They never bothered her. She took them as just another part of life. I wonder who they visit now. It isn't me. I never see any ghostly relatives in my home or at my Sister's house. Perhaps they've shifted their attention to another branch of the family. Or, maybe they do still visit the old house, hoping that someone will be home.

Chapter 2:
Cry Me a River

I'm not sure the first time I heard this story. I was a very young girl because I remember worrying about "the ghost" grabbing my feet when we sat on the footlog and especially when we were in the swimming hole. Creeks are homes to lots of small creatures that like to nibble your feet and legs—minnows, turtles, and bigger fish as well. So you can imagine how nerve-wracking it was being a little girl happily kicking your legs in murky water and then feeling a nibble on your calve or toe.

The dead are all around us. They are in the earth, in the water, in the very air we breathe. When I was a little girl, my grandfather used to tell me about the ghosts on the creek. There were lots of them. There was the Civil War soldier who walked the road from Franklin to here always trying to get home. There was the headless man who stalked the wagon roads mutely holding a lantern in his graying hand. There was the baby who cried shallowly from the walls of the old Milburne cabin—a house that no one had lived in for longer than a year at a time since before my grandfather was a boy. And there was the River Woman. No one knew her name, but most of us, at one time or another, had seen her slow, weeping walk down the banks of the river.

Oh, it's not really a river. We call it that. Most of us have never seen a real river. My grandfather said that he once saw the Mississippi and that it was so far across you couldn't see the other side. Even the Duck River, that has the name, is really only a creek with attitude. Our river was really a creek—a big, fierce creek that became even fiercer after a hard rain, but a creek nonetheless. You could walk across it if you found enough strategically placed stones. It was waist-high in most places, but it ran low in the summer. There were low slick, mossy places that would catch you unawares and sharp rocks that would tear right through a rubber boot. Mean catfish, big as small dogs, lived in the muddy banks, and had been known to take a chunk out of a fisherman's leg. Men had drowned in that creek after floods or when they'd had too much to drink. Little kids had floated away right in their mother's sight when a bad current caught them. Sometimes there were dead things in the creek—cows, birds, and things that water had carried so long that no one could name them. Still, I never knew of any spirit to walk those waters except the Weeping Woman. I've seen her—twice in fact. You can only see her at dusk—right as the sun is coming up or going down. She's not one for starry nights or the light of day. Her hair is the color of birch tree bark, pale brown and white mixed together to form a color not quite gray. She was like a faded picture. Clear, but almost cracked around the edges. Even a fool could see that she wasn't human anymore. It was as if she had tried really hard to remember what someone should look like, but just could quite remember the particulars. She had hands and feet and hair, but they were the merest outlines of a woman. The only thing about her that was whole was her grief. She walked the edge of the water and cried. She cried noisily, the kind of hiccupping sobs that come from the very heart of a person. She never looked up. She never spoke to anyone that I ever heard of. She just walked and cried and left no footprints—not even after a rainstorm when the banks were so muddy-slick that a man only walked near them at his peril.

There's a story about her. No name. Just a story. My grandfather said that his grandfather told it to him. She was a girl that lived at the far end of the creek. There were cabins there once. Now, there's nothing there at all, but a heap of sand that the county pushed up for flood control. She was a plain girl with brown hair and brown eyes. She wasn't beautiful or

7

smart or particularly clever, but everyone agreed she had a good heart. She was the sort of girl that nursed injured animals, even the wildest badgers and foxes, back to health. She patched the broken wings of birds and she sang as she worked. Back then, everyone worked—even the smallest child. On a farm, the work is never done from sun up to sundown. She had rough hands from working the dirt and rough feet from walking barefoot all summer. Her hair, more often than not, had a sprig of hay or rowan in it. Maybe she had dirt on her nose some days or a hole in her calico dress. But, none of that was important. The important part was that she was a good girl. Truly good at heart which was as rare in those days as it is now.

She fell in love with the preacher's son. The preacher, a kind man himself if a little absent-minded, was from up North somewhere. He had attended a swear-to-God seminary school and had a degree to hang on his wall. His house, which was in town, a half-day's ride by wagon or horse, had lace curtains and a real from porch with a swing. His son, a handsome boy, who was fully aware of his good looks, didn't work at all. He kept to his studies—or he was supposed to anyway. Most days, he rode around the county on his fine dark horse causing all sorts of trouble. His friends, equally given to mean-spiritedness and laziness, met up with him when they could. But, most of them were country boys who had cows to milk and fields to plow and couldn't give their selves over completely to dissolution. The preacher's wife, God-rest-her-soul, had passed on some years earlier. By all accounts, she had been a gentle woman with some money to her name. It was because of her, or more specifically her money, that the preacher and his fair-haired son didn't have to spend their days in shop or field. Preaching, in those days, was seldom a full time job. You would often as not to see the same man you saw at pulpit on Sundays humping it through a furrowed field with his old mule on a Monday or pounding out horseshoes as the local blacksmith. But, this Preacher, was a full time preacher—as rare and precious a thing in those days as a silver dollar or a blue moon.

Despite his leisure time, the Preacher didn't seem to have much time to mind his son, who tore about the neighboring farms and fields making mischief. He'd pull down scarecrows just for spite or knock down a fence slat so that your cows would be found wandering dazedly on the creek bank or the road. He was the kind of boy that threw rocks at old dogs and spooked horses for the sport of it. He shot and killed stray cats and deer and left them to rot with no thought for anything but this own desires. I doubt that a boy like that, a selfish boy with his eyes on nothing but his own pleasure, would've ever noticed a brown faced girl with freckles on the bridge of her nose. His eyes were full of town girls with starched crinoline dresses who wore white gloves in summer and spring and carried umbrellas on rainy days. He would've never noticed such a regular girl even if she had been standing right in front of him offering him a glass of cold water on a sweltering day.

Love is a funny thing. It can make the hardest man go weak at the knees or make the most timid of women as brave as any lion. Love can move mountains, so they say, and I don't doubt that it's true. For this girl, an ordinary girl in every way, love was a revelation. Life seemed sweeter for the very presence of it, even if her beloved never looked her way. Knowing that she loved was enough, and she believed, in time, as with all things, love could only turn things to the better. Every time she saw the fair-haired boy—in town, at church, at a barn dance, or along the river, she'd smile and wave. Despite his lack of interest, she hoped that she was an ameliorating influence on him—that somehow her very goodness would rub off on him and he would in the end give up his wicked ways. The girl believed that like the proverbial light on a hill she could cast goodness by the strength of her desire into his black heart. Of course, she didn't believe he was bad through and through. Others might believe that, but she could see in the darkest recesses of his blue eyes that some goodness—some spark of the Divine still lurked there.

Someone with less optimism or more experience would've given up the first time he turned away or when he and his half-drunken friends almost ran her down with a buckboard. But, the girl was one for perseverance. She'd seen that even the wildest of stray cats could, with enough kindness, be taught to eat from your hand. A dog that always bit wasn't naturally mean, just ill-treated. With enough love and patience, any animal could be taught to love. But the preacher's son was no stray cat or bird with a broken wing. He was a man, or close enough to it for the edges of boyhood to be rubbing thin. He wasn't mean due to cruelty done to him, but because of the very cruelty of his own nature. If a dog bit him, it was because he deserved it.

The girl should have known the warning signs—when small children and house pets run, it's because a man's heart is black through and through. Children and animals, so akin to each other, navigate by the standing up of hair on arms, by the feel of the wind. They know the scent of badness as surely as the smell of a rotten apple. Small things don't survive very long if they don't know what's coming around the bend. After a church service, while everyone stood around reviewing the week's gossip and exchanging recipes for apple pies and remedies against bee stings, the fair-haired boy and his friends stalked off to their own fun. Children ran when they saw them. They whispered that even to have one of their shadows fall on you was a sign of ill luck to come. The girl ignored all these stories. She never listened to a bad word said about anyone. Some might think that a good quality in a girl or anyone else—but in this case, there was a reason behind all the talk. There's never smoke without fire, one might say.

Years passed while the girl mooned after the preacher's son. During that time, the girl grew taller and more freckled and her heart grew even softer. So sweet was her nature that bees would follow her scent mistaking her for a flower in bloom. Birds would land on her shoulder when she sat very still and children ran up to her and held her hand without even knowing her name. The fair-haired boy, her opposite in every way, only grew more perverse with time. As his face became more beautiful, his hair more golden, and his eyes the color of the sky after a storm, his heart grew smaller and harder until his soul, if he even had one, was no bigger than a pebble—and certainly no more yielding. He broke a heart a week and thought nothing of it. He drank and rode all night with his friends. Their laughter could be heard echoing in the night like wild riders—and they were just as dangerous to meet on a moonlight stroll. They'd been known to thrown men into freezing ponds for sport and chase children off the road. They ran down small animals and shot anything they could. The fair-haired boy cared for nothing save himself and he could've easily sat by and watched his friends be drowned one by one without shedding a tear.

The girl lived by the creek in a four-room cabin with a wide porch. She liked to sit on the porch late on summer evenings when the mosquitoes had landed for the night and the honeysuckle is sweet and heavy on the air. It was a night just like that, a moist summer night, when she heard the boy crying out. It was the cry of a child and not a man, and at first she thought that some child had fallen in the river. The water was high and swollen with a week's worth of rain. Whitecaps swelled against the bank's edges and caught on rocks. Fallen trees and scree swirled passed giving the water a dull muddy look even at night. The moon was full that night and the girl could see a long way. She could see the boy's friends standing on the bank of the river and she could see the foot log slipping. The boy, dared by his friends, had climbed out on the foot log—a long piece of pine roughly hewn and safe enough in dry weather. But, with the storm, the water brushed the bottom of the foot log making it sway and buck. The boy, as foolish with his own safety as with others, walked whistling out on the wood, but halfway across, the foot log slipped away from the muddy bank and started to be pulled into the furious waters.

The boy had time to cry out and try to run back to his friends before the log slipped into the murky waters. The girl watched as he clung to the log, his bright hair pasted to his face, his eyes wide with fury and fear. With no thought for herself, she waded out into the water, the current pushing against her—her dress twisting against her legs and pitching her forward onto a rock. The boy on the log sailed passed her, one hand out-reached, their fingertips almost touching, and for that one time, he really saw her. He saw her completely. She reached her hands out toward him with all her hope and love, but he slid under the water and was gone. The log swirled by, hitting the bank and gaining momentum, while the girl clung to the rock and cried. She could hear voices, his friends, calling from the bank, but she said nothing. Eventually, someone pulled her out of the water and put her to bed. She developed a fever from the cold water and her own grief, but she was young and soon regained her strength—if not her heart.

They found the boy several miles down the creek. His beauty was gone now, but the girl never saw him. She was too ill to attend the funeral—her fever lasting several days. In her mind, he remained the bright boy laughing with his friends or the desperate one reaching out for her hands

For the rest of her life, the girl loved the fair-haired boy. Death had erased all his faults—not just to her, but to the entire town. In life he had been spoiled and selfish, but in death he was given a kind-heart and a loving nature. The very people who had said he had the devil in him now praised him for his open-handedness and his way with children and animals. Everyone said he loved his mother above all other things, although in life, he had refused to even open a door for her on a cold day. The girl, who was always kind and gentle-natured, only grew more generous and sweet-spirited. Although she was never beautiful, she could sew a fine stitch and everyone loved her. Her goodness drew men to her and several made proposals, but she turned them all down—or rather, she really never noticed them at all. Her eyes were still on the fair-haired boy and her heart was with him always.

She lived a long life, and though she had no children of her own, all children loved her. She grew roses in her garden and was too indulgent to even pull up violets or creeping jennet. She left out crumbs for the birds in winter and milk for stray cats. And, every sunset, she walked the river bank, winter and summer, sun and rain, and thought of the fair-haired boy. It seems that even in death, she still walks and thinks of him. I've seen her, sometimes, in the late shadows, walking with her head down streams of tears falling from her face. She'll pass you with a whisper of air and a faint scent of lavender and rosemary—the herbs that make you think most of loss and might-have-beens. Strangely, no one has ever seen a hint of the boy, drowned though he was, along those dark banks. Perhaps love is what lingers on in the case of the girl—and love, unlike fear or even sorrow, cannot be diminished by time or distance or even death. Who knows? But, she does walk the banks of the river, a brown haired girl watching the waters for a lover that was never hers in life.

Chapter 3:
Long Way Home

My Grandpa took a walk every day at three o'clock in the afternoon. He called it his constitutional, and fair weather or foul he'd get out his hickory and cherry walking stick and set out across the fields. He liked to walk along the farm's perimeter to inspect the fences for wear and storm-damage. Cows are sneaky creatures, who would take even the slightest opportunity to make a run for it.

Sometimes, if I asked, he would take me with him on his walks. But it was cold that particular day, a frosty day in November only a week before the first big snow, and I was already helping my grandmother in the kitchen. My Granny was making teacakes and both she and I had dough up to our elbows as he was preparing for his walk. We heard him say that he'd be back in a bit. We hardly looked up from rolling the vanilla-scented dough when he left.

We finished making the tea-cakes in about an hour. And, after eating two or three each, we decided to start a fire in the big wood stove my grandparents kept in their living room. Granny sent me out to get some kindling and a few stacks of wood. It took me a couple of trips since eight-year-old arms can't carry more than a stick or two at a time. I took my time getting the wood. Sometimes there were mice in the wood-box and I was always leery about sticking my hand inside. I'd reached in and ended up with a handful of mouse more than once.

I could see the first two pastures from the end of my grandparents' porch, but I couldn't see my Grandpa anywhere. Usually, he was only gone half an hour or so. But, I figured he was checking on one of the cows that was about to calf, or that he might be in the barn.

We got the fire going and settled back to look through some old picture boxes. My grandmother must have had ten huge crumbling boxes of pictures. Each box was stuffed with photos of relatives in no particular order. I liked to sort through them all, asking who each one was and placing them in piles on the floor. I grabbed more teacakes and settled down by the pictures, expecting Grandpa to be back any minute. Granny told me to stop stuffing my face with teacakes and warned me that I was ruining my supper.

Granny didn't want to start dinner until my Grandpa was back. If he was looking after one of the cows, it might be a long time before he came back up to the house and everything would be cold by then. I remember sitting on the wood floor sorting through the big box of pictures. Some of them were so old that they flaked to bits when you picked them up, and some were made of tin and had pictures of relatives that lived during the Civil War. I sat on the hard wooden floor waiting and looking at those pictures. Teacake crumbs kept falling in the box and I would have to stop and pick them out. I felt nervous, but I couldn't figure out why. My Granny kept getting up every little bit and looking out the chintz dot curtains on the window above the door. She always kept the big iron key that opened the front door stuck in the keyhole and every time she looked out the window, the key would jangle and make a low rustling noise that sounded like someone trying to get in. Even though we had a fire going and Granny kept adding wood, the room was so cold.

Hours passed, and Granny told me to go and call my Dad come over and look for Grandfather. Granny had a bad knee and couldn't walk very far over the uneven fields even with her cane. She knew she'd never make it up to the far pasture where the cows liked to go when they were about to calf. I tried the phone, but it was busy. So, I decided I'd just run down the road to my house and let my dad know that Grandpa was probably having trouble with one of the cows and Granny wanted to know if he could lend a hand. My dad was in the basement working on his truck when I got there. He said it might be a little while, but that as soon as he got the truck going he could come down and help Grandpa with the cows. I took off back to Granny's house, cutting across the creek. There was ice in places, so I had to be careful not to slip. I was so intent on watching my feet, I never looked up to the fields. I could have seen across them easily from the creek-bank.

When I got back to Granny's house, she was sitting in her big, leather chair with the afghans wrapped around the arms staring at the door. I told her that Dad was on the way in the truck, but she said Grandpa wasn't coming home. "What do you mean?" I asked her, confused and starting to cry for no reason. And, she said, "Your Grandpa's already been here to tell me not to worry and that he's all right, but he won't be coming home." I sat down in the floor then and started crying in earnest, because I knew she meant he was dead.

In about an hour, my dad came up to the house. He'd seen Grandpa sleeping against the fence post like he used to do sometimes on sunny days after he had taken his walk. Dad thought it was a little cold to be napping outdoors, but Grandpa always did exactly what he wanted to do. But, when my father got up to him, he saw that my grandfather wasn't sleeping. The emergency room physician said he probably had a heart attack. Granny told my dad not to worry, that Grandpa had said his last good-byes to her, and that she knew he was in a better place and that everything was fine. I just wish I had been there to see him one last time and to hear his last good-byes to us all.

Chapter 4:
Hollow

"Country people have country ways, and don't you ever forget it," my grandmother used to tell me. I wasn't always sure what that meant. As a child, I was sure that it meant something embarrassing—perhaps having to do with hand-made clothes or lunches brought from home instead of purchased in the yellow-and-green school cafeteria. We used to take long walks on my grandmother's land. Constitutionals, she called them. We'd walk along the creek and past the old barn that lost its top floor in a big wind and was never replaced. We walked through the hay fields with her knocking the tall grass out of the way with her hickory cane. Finally, we'd walk up to the woods to see The Lady.

The Lady wasn't a person, nor was she precisely a thing. She was a tree. An ancient tree. As a child, she was wider around than my arms could reach and my grandmother said she's been just as big when she was a child. The Lady was a beech, smooth-barked with high limbs and leaves the shape of a person's eyes half-closed. She stood deep within my grandmother's property line—past my grandfather's tree stands, past the rusted remains of an old still, past anything that looked kin to man. When you were in the heart of the woods, you could've been anywhere or anytime. The only sounds you could hear were the sounds of the trees and the winds and the animals that passed. Sometimes it was so still you could hear your own breathing as shy and whispery in your ear as a frightened hare.

I can remember standing beneath The Lady, her highest branches far out of reach of my eight-year old eyes and almost forgetting to breathe. We'd always bring her something—shiny stones, a ring of hair tied with a ribbon, a robin's nest found along the way—just something. It seemed disrespectful to visit empty-handed. You never drop by someone's house uncalled without a little something—or so I'd always been taught. You made a welcome for yourself so that next time they'd be glad to open the door even if they didn't look too welcoming this time.

As time went on, I visited The Lady, and indeed, my grandmother less and less. It seemed like I always had something important to do. Lots of things are important to a high school girl and later a woman in college. There were friends to meet, shoes to buy, and boys, always boys. Sometimes though, when the wind moved across my face just right, I'd think of The Lady for no reason. I wonder how the woods looked just then with sunlight or rain or moonlight streaming through the trees. I'd think about how quiet they could get and the way the air tasted like lightning and smoke all at once. I'd think about the low hum the trees could make and the crackle of leaves under my feet, and for a moment or two I'd feel empty and lost. Then, the light would change or the phone would ring and I would forget. Blissfully ignorant and distracted I would go on with all those meaningless and everyday things that can fill up an entire life if you don't pay close attention. I'd do the laundry, watch TV, read a book, and I'd forget. Until I slept, until I dreamed. Sometimes, I'd wake up with a sense of something gone that was so severe that I'd check my arms and legs just to make sure that nothing had fallen off in the night. But, by morning, with a clear light shining through my dorm window and my roommate eating cereal straight out of the box, I'd forget.

It was almost Halloween—the time of the year when the air is as crisp as fallen leaves and you can smell something you can't place almost like cinnamon with every breath. Thanksgiving break falls hard on you that time of year and then Christmas and before you know it, the year has gone and you're up to your neck in another semester of exams and theses and roommates with problems. Every Halloween, we had a big bonfire party to celebrate the almost-end of the semester. Some farmer would be begged or bribed into lending a field still sharp with hay-stubble and it would be ringed out for the autumn fire.

It took nearly two days to build the teepee-like structure that would be the heart of the fire. We'd usually drop by and watch the progress, sometimes lending a hand between classes. The air that time of year still has a hint of moisture in it during the day, but at night, even here in the South, it has a bite. On Bonfire Night I threw on a jacket and my roommate and I, sans boyfriend this time since she and he had a screaming match right outside my door the night before, drove down to the hay field and waited with everyone else for the lighting of the fire.

It was an event. The fire, sometimes reluctant, blazed up on almost the first lighting. The crack of a big fire starting is something to hear—a mixture between a Fourth of July rocket and an old Chevy backfiring. Then, there are the crackles and pops of the fire coming to its own. I've always liked to watch fire—whether it was a candle or a spectacle like this, but somehow standing there with a group of cheering and half-drunk sophomores and seniors seemed empty.

I roamed away from the scene barely feeling my roommate's half-hearted tug on my jacket sleeve towards a little clump of woods nearby. Not a forest—just a little round of trees that someone had left for looks or due to lack of initiative. The trees were mostly pine with a few birches and maples thrown in. Brown needles and leaves crunched under my feet. It had been a hot dry year and the leaves had fallen early. I took off my jacket and tied it around my waist. The air was cool on my arms after the fire, but I didn't care. I leaned my head against one of the bigger pines and was surprised to feel tears on my neck. I put both hands flat on the tree-trunk and wept in earnest. Big flat sobs, nothing that a soap-opera heroine would have ever owned, but tears from the heart.

After a while, it started to rain. I could hear the hoots and screams of those at the bonfire. And, I could imagine their scramble to keep the fire going. The rain was low and gentle. Just sprinkles. As silent and as unobtrusive as a wind through your hair or a pat on the back. The moon was rising above the trees, pushing through the clouds and I noticed it was almost full. The rain cast a ring around it and in its shadow I could see a tree. It stood apart from the others, even in this small space, and it seemed to have strength to it missing from all the others. In the moonlight with the smoke of the bonfire drifting and the rain padding gently, it looked like my tree, my Lady, standing alone in this unforgiving place. I walked toward it, shielding my eyes to look past the rain. It was dead. It was hollow. I could see where lightening had struck it and the tree had rotted away a space big enough for a man. I put my hands on the tree—not the wisest course during a rainstorm—and I wept again. But, this time, I cried not only for myself, but for the tree. I cried for what I was and for what I wasn't. I cried for everything that could've been, and might've been, and might yet be. Eventually, I walked out of the woods. I don't remember it very well, but I ended up in my dorm room under flannel sheets with blue stars.

On Thanksgiving break I went home. I practically ran up my grandmother's porch and flung open the screen door. "Teacakes in the oven," was the only acknowledgement she gave me. I walked into the kitchen and found her at the white enamel sink pulling dough off her fingers.

"I guess you'll be taking a walk," she asked. I nodded. "Been awhile," she said. "Cookies should be out when you get back and cool enough to eat." I put my backpack down on the floor and headed out the back door. It was true autumn now and the air was cold. I pulled my jacket around me. We had already had the first snow of the season and in the hollow frost still clung to low weeds and crunched under my step. In tennis shoes, the climb through the woods was hazardous. I slipped on wet leaves and slid on muddy slopes, but finally I made it to the clearing. There she stood. The Lady. As serene and commanding as ever. I pulled ring from my finger, sterling silver with a claddagh heart and approached her base. Nothing looked wrong, but something felt off-balance. I dropped the ring and ran to her. She was dead. It was lightning. She stood intact, except for the burn mark running down her far side. But, I could see that there was no life in her.

I sat down in the dead leaves and covered my face with my hands. Then I felt it. A small brush against my leg. It was a cat. A kitten, really, no bigger than my hand. I picked her up and looked around for others, but she was alone. Tiny, big-eyed, with white and silver fur, she brushed her tiny head against me with a strength beyond her size. I scooped her up and wrapped her in my jacket.

When I got back to the house, I could smell vanilla and molasses when I opened the door. A tray of cookies sat on the wood-burning stove. "Still hot," my grandmother said.

"Did you know?" I asked still panting a little from my run and clutching the cat in my jacket. She nodded. "Yep," she said, "happened a while back. Wasn't nothing to be done for her." She picked up a cookie and bit into it. I put the kitten down and she began walking with high-steps around the living room finally hopping onto the couch and circling herself into a sleep. We watched her until she was still.

"I wish I could've done something," I said. "I feel guilty." But, I knew as soon as I said it that it wasn't true. I felt better and more complete than I had in a long time. She finished the cookie and took a drink of tea. "Some things happen, that's all," she said. "She had a good long run and I guess it suited her well enough."

"I thought she'd always be there," I said. Grandma nodded, "Seems that way, sometimes, but I guess she needed a change." I nodded and picked up a cookie. "There weren't any sprouts," she continued. "I checked."

21

"That's odd," I said. Grandma just shrugged and looked at the cat. "None that I saw anyway," she picked up another cookie, "It's hard waiting for visitors sometimes. Might be nice to visit a bit yourself." The cat turned over in her sleep and made a tiny sound almost like the whistle of wind through leaves. I picked up a cookie and took a bite. The kitten slept on.

Chapter 5:
Roses from Thorns

The kitten, Pepper, lived to be twenty-two years old, which is a good long life even for a Siamese cat known for their longevity. She was feisty right up the end, never failing to put an uppity kitten or a dog with ambitions in his or her place. This next story is a bit of a conclusion to "Hollow."

For the first twenty-two years of Pepper's life she had been well, with one exception. When she was two, one of my sister's wild pitches hit her while she was lying behind the catcher's plate. I remember how frightened I was as my mother drove us to the vet's office. Pepper's big blue eyes kept opening and closing frantically. But she ended up with no more than a concussion and the lesson not to lie behind a catcher's plate.

In February of her twenty-second year Pepper was very sick. We had adopted a kitten, Tig, who came down with a case of the sniffles. Unfortunately, a case of the sniffles is a much more serious affair for an older cat and Pepper developed full-blown kitty flu. She had to be injected with fluids twice per day for two weeks and it took her fully a month to recover. In the meantime, she had lost 1/3 of her body weight. Every night I slept with her in my arms and prayed she wouldn't die.

By April, Pepper was ready to lie in the garden again and roll in her favorite patch of lemon balm. She liked to watch the birds dive out of the trees and onto the bird feeder and she still chattered at squirrels when they were brave enough to drop down into her garden. Spring was always been Pepper's favorite time of year. She liked the way the herbs smelled in my garden when they first came up. She used to rub her head on every branch of bee balm and lavender that she saw and pull the blossoms off the catnip.

When I came home from work on April 28, I put my purse on the counter and changed shoes so I could take Pepper outside for her afternoon in the garden. My husband was home that day and I asked him how Pepper was feeling that day, and he said that she had spent most of the day out on the deck lying in the sun-patches. I went into my room and Pepper was lying on her favorite calico cushion. She meowed at me and got up so I could rub her head, but she promptly fell over on her side. I picked her up and ran screaming into the living room. I wrapped Pepper in my jacket and we rushed to the vet's office, but when we were about half way there, I asked Scott to turn the car around. Pepper was dying. I didn't want her to die on some sterile table. I wanted her to be in the garden she loved.

Pepper died on April 28, in her garden in my arms. I buried her in our family pet cemetery beside her sister, Licorice, who had died two years earlier. Putting her tiny box in that freshly dug hole was the emptiest feeling I've ever had. I had Pepper with me twenty-two years of my life, and I could scarcely remember a time before her. She and her sister, Licorice, ran and fought and played through my earliest childhood memories. I couldn't remember a time without Pepper, a day without hearing her low purr or feeling her brush against my ankles.

I spent that night sobbing into my pillow. Pepper always slept on that pillow and I could still smell her cinnamon-y smell. Sometimes, I thought I could hear her nails walking across my wooden floors. For a month, I barely slept or ate and I still called out Pepper's name each time I came through the front door. I couldn't help but look for her every time under every rose bush and clump of lemon balm when I weeded the garden.

One rainy morning in May, I woke up I opened up the deck door by habit so that Pepper could go outside. Tig promptly ran onto the deck and started mewing in that crazy off-key way that Maine Coons have. I thought a bird or squirrel might have fell onto the deck the way Tig was carrying on; but when I walked outside, the smell of roses hit me. Ever rose bush in my garden was blooming. Roses that had been weeks away from budding had bloomed in the night. And, underneath the wild rose bush in my garden was a tiny Siamese kitten. She was wet from the night's rain and meowing piteously.

I ran down to the garden and scooped up the shivering kitten. She was no bigger than my hand. I wrapped her in my sweater and brought her inside to meet Tig. The two had a bit of a rocky start, but they became fast-friends in a week or two. Nonny, my new kitten, has been with me for almost a decade now. I can't help but believe that Pepper sent her to me seeing how much I needed a new friend.

There are so many things about Nonny that remind me of Pepper—her grace, her polite little meow, the way she loves the garden, and her insatiable love of lavender. But I miss Pepper every day as well. I miss the way she used to purr into my throat when she slept on my chest and the way her little toenails click-clicked on my floors. I miss the way she used to roll on any sweater that fell on the floor and I miss finding the tiny chewed catnip mice. Most of all, I miss her sweet self. Now whenever I smell the spring roses in my garden, I think of my kind Pepper-cat; but I also think of Nonny and I'm grateful for both.

Chapter 6:
First Semester

She had the same schedule as me. Whether I took the trash down before classes at 7:00 AM or after work at midnight, she would always be there in the hallway. In the beginning, I thought it strange that I never saw her on campus or in one of the many general studies classes that Freshman are inevitably forced to take before they declare their majors. But it was a big campus and some people just like to keep to themselves. I know I did.

Potter Hall was the only building left standing from the original Potter Normal School for Teachers. The rest of the campus was mostly new and brick with pseudo-Greco columns and English ivy. But Potter Hall was Victorian whitewashed with crumbling interiors and radiators that burned so hot you had to open your windows even the dead of winter. Potter Hall was three stories with one window in every room and two for the rooms on the ends. Two dirty green dumpsters used to sit in parking lot within a stone's throw from the building. Unfortunately, students quickly learned that they were also within a heavily-laden garbage bag's throw as well. After a couple of professors and students were pelted by near-misses, campus authorities decided to move the dumpsters into Potter Hall on the bottom floor. The garbage chutes that had been used in the 1940-60s had long ago been boarded up. So students had to lug their trash bags down to the basement of Potter and leave them in the "garbage room."

Needless to say, a trip to the "garbage room" was usually confined to once per week and only when every possible trash receptacle was stuffed. I was luckier than most, since I had an extra trashcan. My roommate had decided not to return after spring semester, leaving me with a private room. It also made me the sole person responsible for trips to the dreaded "garbage room." The smell usually hit you on the third or fourth stair down. It was worse in the summer and on rainy days, but it wasn't exactly a picnic in the winter. The trick was to run down the stairs, kick open the door to the garbage room, throw your bags from the door, and run back up the stairs as quickly as possible. I usually made my trash run at night, after the first round of studying and before the second pot of coffee.

It was October the first time I noticed her. At first, I thought she was a reflection of me. The bottom floor of Potter Hall had once been dorm rooms during Potter's Normal School past. There were mirrors, albeit dirty and sometimes cracked ones, at the end of each hallway. I had just thrown my trash bags into the dumpsters (almost landing both bags in the green monstrosities) and was preparing to let the door slam when I caught a bit of movement out of my left eye. I turned and saw her standing at the end of the hallway. She looked like me. Dark hair, pale skin, the look of a habitual coffee-drinker. She even had on darkish clothing, which I preferred at the time. I gave her a jaunty little salute in the way of a hello and ran back up the stairs as quickly as possible. I had a test in French Composition in the morning and was dressed in ragged sweats and a scrunchie. I was not in the mood or attire to strike up new acquaintances.

Only once I was back in my book-strewn room did I think that it was odd that she had been coming to the garbage room from the other end of the hallway. The only way to the trash room that I knew was down the stairs and to the left. She had been coming from the opposite end of the building. I vowed to look for another passage the next trash day. Hopefully, it would be shorter and not involve running up and down a narrow flight of peeling stairs.

A week passed and trash day was upon me. I twisted my two bags closed and got ready for the run down the stairs. The girl wasn't there that day. I checked once I had tossed my bags and let the door slam, blocking off some of the smell. I looked to the left—no girl and no light. "God," I thought, "she must have some nerve to drag trash bags through the dark, even if it is a short cut!" The bottom floor windows, what few there were, had been boarded over long ago. Abandoned windows make too convenient targets for rock-hurling freshman guys. I decided that I would try to determine her way in from outside the building, Nancy Drew-style, and with a flashlight the next day.

So, a couple of weeks passed. Okay, I know I said the next day, but there were things to study and papers to write, not to mention concerts to see and cookies to eat. Anyway, I finally remembered around the beginning of November that there was another way into the basement of Potter. I had seen the girl once since then, but she was far down the hall in the dark and when I yelled at her she didn't answer. I wasn't about to go chasing after her. I figured if she didn't want to chat there was no crime in that.

The next day after my classes were over, I went to my room, got a flashlight, and prepared to circle Potter looking for an entrance. I found broken windows, chipped bricks, and finally a green door. It was securely locked, padlock and everything. So I thought she must be a Resident Advisor. They had keys to everything and I only knew the RA on my own floor. There were three more in Potter alone. I decided to ask Eve, my RA, if there was a shortcut through the basement. She told me there wasn't and that I should stay out of the basement except for trash-dumping purposes. She gave me several reasons: I could fall, a rat might bite me, and several other terrible scenarios that Resident Advisors are compelled to tell freshman to keep them out of trouble.

The third week in November, I screwed up my nerve and decided to check out the basement head to toe, trusty flashlight in hand, of course. No trash-flinging pretense this time, I descended the stairs and walked past the trash room. No girl was in sight. I thought I saw a glimmer of light toward down the hallway, though. "Ah-ha!" I thought, "So this is her secret way in!" I would like to say I ran toward the glimmer, but actually, I kind of crept. The floor was dirty and not everyone bothered to get their trash all the way into the dumpsters. So, I kind of side-stepped my way down the hall, eyes open for those rats the RA had so kindly warned me about.

There was a glimmer of light. Seemingly from inside one of the dorm rooms. "Could she be actually staying down here?" I wondered. I couldn't imagine anyone would hate their roommate so much that they'd have to escape to the smelly basement, but who knew? Anyway, I thought for sure that the door would be locked, but it pushed open easily enough. The switch was off, but the room was somewhat light. I can't really explain it. While it wasn't as bright as if the light had been on, it wasn't the pitch-black of no light bulbs that the rest of the basement had. I could see in that room. No one was there, but I could see.

The room was empty. No furniture. No drapes. Windows boarded. Just what you would expect to find in the basement of Potter Hall. Flashlight down, I walked around. No light coming from under the boards at all. I was looking at the window boards when I thought I saw movement out of the corner of my eye. I turned and nothing was there. So, I left the room pulling the door closed behind me. When I closed the door the hallway was black again. But, just before I closed the door, I thought I had seen something metallic catch my flashlight's light. I shined it around. There was a plaque outside the door. I trained my flashlight on it and read: *In Memory of Evelyn.* "Weird," I thought, "dedicating flagstones and benches are all the rage, but you never see a dedicated room!" I headed back toward the stairs.

When I reached the trash room, I felt, I don't know, compelled to turn back. You know that feeling you get when the hairs on your arm stand up and you feel a little ball of cold

29

the size of a walnut right under your navel? Anyway, I looked back down the hall and there she was, in front of the door. Just standing. I yelled "Hey!" at her, but she didn't respond. This time I did run down the hall after her, but about mid-way, my flashlight gave out. I stopped and gave it a good pounding, but by the time that it was working again, she was gone.

The next day, I decided to look up Evelyn out of curiosity. There had to be something about the room's dedication in the college newspaper. Sure enough, a name search on the newspaper's microfiche archives gave me four articles. I read them in chronological reverse, since that's the way they were filed. The last two were about the dedication of the room in 1945. Evelyn's parents had left the university a substantial amount of money on the condition that the room always bears the plaque. I don't suppose they ever thought it would end up adjacent to the trash room. The third article mentioned a scholarship Evelyn's parents had set up in her name. But, the last was Evelyn's obituary. It had a picture. The picture of a pale girl with dark hair wearing a dark shirt and skirt. The skirt was a little long, but it was exactly what was in fashion in 1943. I continued living in Potter Hall for three more years, but I never saw her again.

There are actually lots of ghost stories about Western Kentucky University. I worked at the Kentucky Museum my freshman and sophomore years and it had a ghost of its own with a sense of humor. He liked to give new employees a good scare, but left the old hands alone. If the museum was quiet, you could hear footsteps in the Victorian section that would echo around the room and then slowly move down the hall. The elevator also made little journeys on its own and hung at odd floors. As you can imagine, we mostly took the stairs.

After my second semester, Potter Hall was converted to an administrative building. I've always wondered if the ghost preferred the building as dorms or if she liked the quieter office atmosphere.

Chapter 7:
Choose Your Partner

I have always heard that the air is cold when spirits are present. That may be true for some people, but I have never experienced it for myself. When I walked into my room at Talbot's Tavern, the air was dry and hot. Someone had turned the air conditioning unit down to its lowest setting. I immediately adjusted it to 70 and felt the cold air hit me with a jolt. I was already hot and tired—a crumpled mess after having ridden several hours in the car. One of my husband's childhood friends was getting married tomorrow, so we had decided to make a trip of it, reserving a few nights in a historic hotel. Talbot Tavern, despite having two fires and several renovations, still maintained the ambience of an 18th century tavern. The white-bricked outer walls were wound with ivy and wisteria and the window panes had the heavy-paned waved glass of Colonial America.

I collapsed on the canopied bed, plopping my suitcase and duffel bag on the floor. "I'm about to drop," I said lying on the bed with my hanging suit-bag draped across me like a comforter. "Well," said my husband, "It's only three hours until the reception dinner." I rolled on the bed in complaint. "I'm going downtown," he said, "to see if I can find some film for the camera. I don't suppose you want to come with me?" I threw my hand over my eyes dramatically, and was rewarded with the sound of the door closing as he left. I got up, hung the suit-bag on the shower curtain rail and curled up under the white-knobbed afghan for a good sleep. I don't know how long I slept, but I awoke suddenly—the way you do when you hear a sharp noise or a baby's cry. From the light falling through the window, I knew it must be close to sunset or maybe a little after dusk. Motes of dust danced on the air and the room felt heavy. The windows were closed but I could smell something sweet, like honeysuckles after a rain-storm or roses crushed underfoot. I looked around; the door to the hallway was still closed and everything looked the same as I had left it.

I opened the door and went down the hallway. Leaning over the spiral stairwell in the center of the upstairs parlor, I could see the bustle of the lobby below and smell food from the dining room. No one else was in the hallway or the parlor, so I decided to go sit on one of the swings on the outside balcony. The heavy door leading to the balcony creaked when I opened it and a rush of hot, sticky air hit me. I hung off the balcony and watched the people in the street—mostly summer tourists laden with cameras, diaper bags, and small dogs. Someone was watching me. I spun around, but I couldn't see anyone in the hallway. I opened the door and stepped back inside, but no one was there. I called out. No answer. Still, I had the distinct impression that I was not alone. I walked back down the hallway to my room and pushed open the door. No one was there. Half-asleep as I was, I thought maybe I was nervous about the wedding or still groggy from my long car ride. I decided I would take a shower.

I grabbed my bath things and my dress for the reception dinner, a long pale sundress that swept the floor, and went into the bathroom. After a steamy shower, I put on my dress and make-up and went into the main room to find my shoes. The floral smell was even stronger, as was the feeling of being watched. I opened the window with some effort, causing a small bird to vacate a chink in the brick where she had been nesting. Startled, I pulled back from the window into the room. The hot air from outside mingled with the heavy flower scent and I felt dizzy. I could hear, no, almost hear, music. It was light and melancholy. I swung myself around and my full skirt flared as if caught by a wind. I felt something dry brush my cheek like a feather. The music was louder now, but still faint. I stood still and smelled the flowers and heard the music of

33

another era, and I did the only thing I could do. I lifted my right hand and clasped the air and then I danced. Eyes closed, feet bare, skirt swirling in rhythm, I danced. My hand, starting empty and grasping air, soon felt another hand, and I was guided around the room for I don't know how long—until the door opened, the music stopped, the air was still.

"You're already dressed," my husband said, "Good, we need to go down to the reception dinner and I thought you'd still be asleep." I nodded. "I'm ready," I said, and down the stairs we went to dinner. Later, we found out that we were the only guests staying upstairs this weekend. "Don't be surprised if you hear knocks and doors slamming in the night though," the hostess warned me with a smile. "We have a few resident ghosts." Of course, I already knew that—just as I also knew that one of them was a very good dancer.

Talbot Tavern and Bardstown have as many ghost stories as they have buildings. It's a beautiful town and Talbot Tavern is a jewel. You should visit it if you ever have an opportunity. Even if you don't get a chance to dance with a ghost, they bake some mean biscuits and they have a live band most nights if you have a mind to move your feet with a partner.

Chapter 8:
Stone Walls

I wrote this about a law office where I worked for several years in Bowling Green, Kentucky. The office was in a building built in the 1800s. It was a beautiful old building, but a challenge when it came to heating, cooling, and storage. The library had been converted into an office with two desks. I was stationed at one, scribbling and researching away all day. The chimney, which was uncapped, had an unpleasant tendency to drip in bad weather and if you were working late at night, especially if you were the only one in the building, you could sometimes hear this little sighing noise come from the corner of the library. Most people attributed it to the chimney—most of them.

The dead walk here within these walls. I know it's a bit hard to believe, just looking at this place. New, Berber carpeting on all the old, oak floors. Bright strips of fabric wallpaper with rich mosaic designs in every office and a ficus tree in every nook. They may be plastic, those little trees, but I do think they cheer up the place a bit. Looking around, you could almost forget that this building is over two centuries old. That's right – you can check the little metal sign above the entry: 1799.

The bones, as they say, of this building are old. And even though they try with their re-decorating, office lighting, and mood music, they've never been quite able to hide the chill that is always in the air. There's a cold here that isn't a result of the central air and a sadness that isn't caused by overtime hours, if you get my meaning. As we sit and work, eat our lunches and tally our sums, the dead watch over us. *They* sit with us. *They* watch our every move with passivity and what I've come to hope is disinterest. But, is it? What do *they* think, the gray forms that drift through the newly refurbished halls of this old place? Do *they* notice the changes that have taken place over the years? Do *they* stare at our computer screens and wonder what it all means? Or, are *they* so wrapped in their own existence, their own sorrows, that they see nothing at all?

You can't speak with *them*. I've tried. I've been warned not to—told that it wouldn't do any good. It's something the staff will tell you the first day you arrive. Oh, it's not exactly in the orientation packet, but the other workers will tell you all the same—on the sly—like I'm telling you now. *They'll* watch you. Sometimes *they'll* even follow you down a hall, sit in a chair, act like they want to say something, but it's no good trying. You can't speak with the dead. You can't quite reach *them*. There are plenty that have tried. Those people all either leave or change—if you get my drift. They change their minds about it pretty quick if they're going to stay.

You can't just go around trying to talk with *them*. The best thing to do, the thing I do, is to pay *them* no mind. Just because you see the spirit of a soldier standing by your filing cabinet doesn't mean you have to notice him, right? Just leave *them* alone and *they'll* leave you alone. We all rub along just fine here—the living and the not-so-living. It'll start to be in the time that you can't really tell the difference. There's some days, I can tell you, that I'd rather have one of *them* in my office than a fellow flesh and blood co-worker. *They* don't steal your stapler. *They* don't drink the last of the coffee and then not start another pot. And *they're* not always leaving things in the refrigerator for months and months. I mean, why do you bring it if you're not going to eat it, right? It makes no sense.

The one thing about *them* is that they're reliable. *They're* always here. *They* never call in a sick day—no point really. *They* don't forget an appointment or a birthday—because *they* don't remember them at all. *They* don't forget to give you memos, or gossip about you behind your back. *They're* just about the best office mates you can find, really. There's some that'll tell you that you're unlucky being stuck here in the library with me. Those folks that don't like it in here—they say it gives them a creepy feeling just coming through the door.

I hear them, of course, what they say. But let me tell you, it might be a little damp in here from time to time—but that's because of the chimney. The office won't pay to have it capped even though we don't use it, and last year water came flooding down when we had that big rain. What do they care anyway? It's just me—and you—and *them* here, right? You see, *they* like it here. Back in the day, before this building was an office, mind you, back during the War, the place was used as a hospital. And this was the room, they say, where the dead were put. There was a little cart that was rolled in and used to load the bodies up for transportation to the morgue at night. That's what I was told anyway. I never saw it, of course. That was years and years ago.

It is said that before this old place was restored, the basement had an earth floor and that the walls down there were stone. All the upper floors were wood, and I guess they would've liked to keep them, but it was too expensive to replace all the oak and stuff stained as it was. You can't paint over it, you know—blood. It seeps right through. Nothing can get it out once it's in—just like *them*, that way. And the stones too, they say, just draw it up. Every chink and crack. You can't get that kind of thing out.

I know there're some that'll say I'm a bit cracked myself for saying this, but I think that's the way of it all around. I don't know if you believe in ghosts, spirits, or what have you, but you'll come to believe something once you see a few of *them*. Everyone has their own explanation, whatever makes them feel the most comfortable. Most say they don't see anything. But here's what I think, if you ask my opinion. I think that there's only so much sorrow that anything, any place can take. I think when there's suffering been had like this place has seen, that, well, it settles in the very bones of the place. I think the stones themselves would cry out, if they could. But, that's the pity and the sorrow of stone, it can't say a word. So it just goes on and so do *they*.

They just go on day after day the way *they* were and there's nothing to be said or done about it. I try to be kind. I try not to stare. I don't like to be stared at so why should *they*. I know it's a bit of a shock now, I can see by the way that you're looking at me, but you'll get used to it in time. I have noticed that you're not much of a talker and that's good, too. I'm used to the quiet here by now. I like to finish my calculations right before lunch. Then lunch at 11:00, and a bit of filing for the rest of the afternoon. I don't take breaks; don't hold with such things. There's some that have said I should have more fun, take a little time off like the others, but I don't see why. I like the library and the quiet. I don't mind *them* and they don't mind me. And I can see by the way that you've gotten right to work that'll we'll get along just fine, too. I mean, just because you're my replacement doesn't mean we can't get along.

I guess I can help you some, train you up proper as they say. There's no reason for us not to get along. I know I would've liked a little help when I was just getting settled into this position. My current situation is no reason for us not to rub along just fine. Even though you can't exactly hear me, I can tell you know I'm here. I'm not like the others.

I'll just keep to my numbers, same as I did last week and the week before. There's really no reason not to keep at them forever. And maybe, in time, we can both train the next guy.

I see that you take lunch at your desk and that you don't leave any crumbs. I admire that. And I see that you skipped that Susan's birthday party. No call for parties on work time. You're a nose to the grindstone kind of fellow. I like that. I'll just keep to my work and you keep to yours and the dead will follow along as they always do.

38

I made sure to give that Thomas a good scare when he came in here earlier. He was after your stapler or a pen at least—probably one of your favorites. Those others show no consideration. *They're* not the type to respect a good day's work. Most of them didn't even turn up at my funeral. And I'm sure they would never stay around to make sure the audit gets done proper. But I see that you and I are likeminded individuals. Don't mind that fellow in the corner, I can see he gave you a start. He's just doing his job, too. It's the work that matters. In the end, that's what a fellow really is.

This is the kind of place that becomes like a home. In time, you'll probably not want to leave either. I spent most of my time here from morning to night and sometimes to morning again when there was a big audit or a problem with the numbers. I have to admit that I never even knew I was one of *them* until I tried to run the coffeemaker and my hand went right through it. Must have just passed on checking the spreadsheets for the monthly expense reporting. Well, it didn't seem to be a reason to go on. I mean, it's not like I needed a sick day or anything, if you get my meaning.

Here I am. Just like always for the last thirty years. Good old Smithy, they'll say. He sticks to his work. Not too social. Well, to each his own, I say. And maybe if this all goes well, in twenty or thirty or even forty years or so, I'll have the pleasure of addressing you face to face—or person to person—you get my meaning just the same, I'm sure. This is really a wonderful place. A place you can make a home. I have to say that I'm glad, really glad, to meet you. It may take a bit of time to adjust, but you'll get the hang of it. I can tell you're a bright fellow. Don't mind the cold. You'll get used to that, too.

Chapter 9:
Reader's Choice

There is someone in the library. I distinctly hear the sound of soft bare feet on the wooden floor and the slow scrape of a book being removed from the bookcase. I've heard it before—sometimes in the early morning and sometimes at night. I never see anyone in the library. But often books fall mysteriously from the shelf. Sometimes there are stacks of books left in the floor—always in the neat little piles. It is easy to convince myself that I removed the books myself while dusting and forgot to reshelf them. I hear footsteps again. If you live in a house long enough, you'll start to know every little sound—the settling of the roof in autumn, the tapping of limbs against an eave, the creaking of floorboards that comes with age, and the sound of someone walking politely in your library. I should go and look, I know, but I've run to the library and flicked on the light often enough to know that I won't see anything. There may be books piled in the floor, but no one will be there. I'll have just enough time to walk back to the kitchen, fix a soda, and plop down on the couch before I hear the rustle of pages turning or the sly little steps again.

My cats don't seem to mind—except for Mooshie. Mooshie sees something the others don't. Sometimes she stares silently at a corner of the room, tail held high, black fur bristling. She doesn't hiss or growl. She just stares. No one else sees anything. Lady, my patient cocker spaniel, has plopped down right on top of the spot that Mooshie is staring at without flicking an eyelid. The books especially disturb Mooshie. If she finds them on the floor, she gives them a wide berth. She doesn't avoid the library. She lies in the window to catch the morning rays or lounges on top of the toy chest. I think she and my little invisible reader have some sort of understanding.

I've noticed that my mystery reader seems to prefer children's books. I have a large collection. Some are left over from my childhood, but others I've collected over the years for their bright covers. Some were favorites of mine from elementary school or our local library. I have two bookcases of them. My little reader seems to also prefer the lower shelves. One time, all the pillows from the big sofa chair in the corner were pulled onto the floor and a little pile of books were left by its side. Maybe my reader took a nap and forgot to reshelf them.

I never see my little reader. It's been over ten years since we moved into the house. Although Mooshie seems to "see" things in other rooms, things are only moved in the library. I've asked my neighbors about the previous occupants of our house, but there's been nothing out of the usual in our house's history. It's not very old—it was built in the 1970s. No one has ever died here. No one has ever had a serious accident here. There doesn't seem to be any trauma associated with the house or our usual suburban neighborhood, and yet, I have a ghost in my library. A seemingly happy ghost, but a ghost none the less.

The UPS guy has apparently seen her. Yes, it's a her, according to him. But I sort of figured that from her reading choices. One day when I answered the door to pick up a package he told me that my daughter had looked out the library window at him. He said it was smart that she didn't answer the door for strangers. She seems to have good taste in books as well. I found *Anne of Green Gables* on the floor this morning. Last week, it was *Treasure Island* and *The Littlest Witch*. I don't have children, although I do have a pile of cats. I've always wanted a daughter. Maybe she knew she'd be welcome here. Maybe she looked around for a good library before she settled in. I wonder if she visits the public library down the street, as well. I'll have to ask if they ever find books on the floor of the children's section pulled after hours. Regardless,

I'm glad of my little reader—whoever she is. She's welcome to the books and the run of the library.

I haven't seen in book stacking in a few years, but I do still find things moved around in my library. The cats seem particularly interested in the room—all except for Mooshie, my black cat. She will stare into the room and then take off down the hall like her tail's on fire about twice a week, just to come creeping back down the hall to stare in again.

Chapter 10:
Flight & Other Possibilities
of the Human Spirit

When I was six years old I flew from the top step of our house and landed on one outstretched toe graceful as any bird. I remember the way the air whistled around me and the slight tingling as my bare foot touched grass. In ran into the kitchen to tell my mother yelling, "I flew—right off the steps!" She looked up from the bowl, her hands deep in cookie dough, "You jumped," she said, "You're lucky you didn't skin your knee or worse."

"No, no," I said bobbing my head like a duck, "I flew. I did!"

She started kneading the dough again, "Don't let me catch you jumping off the porch again," she said. I think I left then. I tried flying every day for three months after that, but I never managed it again. I did skin my knee, and one day I chipped a tooth. I still dream of it—flying. It did happen. Of course, no one believed me. No one believes me now, and I can just feel you shaking your head. Girls don't fly. Maybe they do in movies, but regular freckle-nosed, grass in their hair, Band-Aid kneed girls don't fly. They jump, they fall, and they go running back inside teary-eyed hoping for a cookie.

Lots of things in my childhood were like that. They fell into two clear camps—things that happened and things that didn't happen—even if they really did. If you heard neighbors fighting and then you saw a bruised arm, you looked away. Good neighbors mind their own business. They mow their lawns and keep their dogs on their own property. If you see a man sobbing on the street, tears falling silently, mouth open with a grief too big to bear, you move along. "Don't stare. We all have our own loads," my Granny would say, "God never hands out more than a man can carry." Bad things sometimes happen. Houses burned, jobs were lost, and everyone rallied to help. The Church would hold a raffle to raise money or everyone would donate their old clothes and toys. If there was a death, there were casseroles to make and Bundt cakes—half chocolate and half white. Those were things that could be faced. They could be dealt with and put to rest. But, other things were tucked away, like quilts for winter circled in lavender and lemon balm to keep the moths out. Things too big or too hard were just forgotten. Time heals all wounds or so they say.

There was a sinkhole on my Granny's land. It was a great and unfathomable mystery to all us kids. You could fill it up with brush and in a day or a week it would be gone. None of us ever saw it do any sinking, but it wasn't from lack of trying. We'd feed the hole leaves and rocks, and once I fed it one of my sister's dolls in a fit of spite. Folks said it would take anything in time. No one ever said where these things went. I asked. No one knew. But it ate things besides sticks and brush and big-eyed plastic dolls.

One day, as I sat cat-quiet underneath the honeysuckle bushes hoping to see something sink, Sandra Clay came and stood by the hole's edge. She looked like she might throw herself in—something not even the bravest of my cousins would dare. Sandra was fourteen to my eight and had sad, blonde-brown hair. She wore glasses and smiled at me when I giggled in Church. She stood looking down into the hole for the longest time and then said in a voice mouse-small but resolute, "I love Billy Marcum, but he doesn't love me. He'll never love me." She stood a little longer and I thought I could almost hear the plop-plop of tears falling into that hole. Then she left.

And she was right. Billy Marcum never did love her. He married a red-haired woman from up North that he met while he was in college. I don't know what happened to Sandra. She moved away after she graduated high school. But I do know that she seemed somehow happier or at least less run-down after that day at the sinkhole. I wondered over the years, how many other women and men stood over that hole pouring down their grief. Many—maybe too many. One day, when I was nearly grown, the sinkhole stopped drawing things down. Brush piled up and eventually, my Uncle used the Ditch Witch to fill it in. "Everything's got a core," my Granny said, "That one's full." Maybe it was filled with all those tree limbs and rocks. But I think there's only so much sadness anything can bear—even a hole.

Sinkholes have always fascinated me. We have quite a few of them in Tennessee and Kentucky. In fact, a rather large one opened up in one fellow's yard just last week in Fairview. Underneath the "hole" was a cavern with several rooms. The fellow was naturally upset, as were his neighbors. You never know what's under the earth or when it might reveal itself.

Chapter 11:
Country Matters

This story was inspired by one I heard around a bonfire. The lady telling it was from Texas, but had moved to Tennessee. Apparently, sheep don't do well in Tennessee as compared to Texas which has one of the largest populations of sheep in the US—although California runs a close second. She said that her family had kept sheep for several generations and that depending on where you live, wolves could be a problem.

I'd never heard that there were wolves in Texas. My sister lived in Texas for several years and never mentioned wolves. This lady went on to tell me that fifty years back, when her grandfather was running a farm, wolves weren't uncommon in Texas and that they had both gray and red wolves. It was nothing for wolves to take a sheep a week if you didn't keep a close watch on your flock. There were folks that specialized in dealing with wolves, and these "wolf-whisperers" were in high-demand despite their quirks.

Used to be that we didn't have much trouble with our flocks around here. Sure, we'd lose a sheep or two to the winter, or falling down a ravine, or sometimes even to wild dogs. But, nothing like this. Nobody's seen anything like this since the times of my great-grandfather—maybe even further back than that, and I'm not a spring chicken these days. Last month I lost three lambs to the wolves. Doesn't seem like too much, but I only have a few hundred. Lose three or four each month and you've lost close to fifty by the year's end. And I'm not the only one. Ranchers up and down this valley have been complaining. Nothing much to be done, apparently. Can't shoot 'em, can't trap for the things. Besides, trapping would catch as many lambs as wolves, I guess. Sheep aren't the smartest animals on this earth, but they still don't deserve to be torn apart by wolves. Fencing doesn't do much good either. Wolves are smart as dogs—smarter maybe. They can slink under a fence quick as anything.

I was in a pickle. I'd tried watching the sheep more, but it's hard work and I don't really have the manpower. I tried getting more dogs, but dogs aren't stupid and any self-respecting dog'll take off with a wolf pack on its heels. But a neighbor of mine said to try the Old Culley Place. Swore by it, he did. Said the Old Woman'd given him a remedy a few years ago that had kept the wolves off his place ever since. I can't say I believed it. I mean, witches, in these days. Seems like something out of an old movie or a fairytale. We have satellite dishes and John Deere around here. And though some say the *Old Farmer's Almanac* is only one step above witchery, well, I still buy one every year. Though, it's more fluff than it was in the past. Too many ads now and all that flower gardening nonsense. Anyway, I was at my rope's end, so I figured, what's the harm in seeing.

Now, the Old Culley Place is not so easy to get to. You can take the state highway up to Grange Road, but once you hit it, you're on pure dirt and gravel. That's bad enough on sunny days, but in the mud or snow, it's a job even for a four wheel drive. Of course, the Old Woman wouldn't care, I figured. She never went anywhere that I knew of. She had her groceries delivered in bulk from town. Let the delivery trucks and UPS hassle with that horrible road, I guess was her thought. She was the Old Woman when I was a boy, and it's been years since I was called anything except Old Farmer Craig or Old Man Craig.

Well, anyway, I got my dog, Clover—I don't go anywhere without her—and fired up the truck for a day trip. Figured I might hit the Co-op on the way back through town. I'd heard they had some new hybrid seeds that were worth having. Anyway, me and Clover hitched in and made the drive in less than two hours—most of it spent navigating pot-holes on Grange Road. It wasn't even lunch yet when we saw the Old Culley Place looming up ahead. Old Miss Culley was always known for a cook, and I was hoping for something to eat, I don't mind telling you. Driving in dust is hard work. So, it was a more than welcome sight to see the old farmstead, neat and as kept as it was when I was a boy. The flower beds even looked good—if you care for that kind of thing. And, I always liked these better than most laid out wild as they were and not in neat little rows like the houses in town. I could smell lavender and rosemary on the air, which is better than red dust any day. The barn lay off to the side and I could see a couple of old cows lazing about. Miss Culley never kept much stock—just a few cows and a fat old horse that I doubt ever saw a plow or a saddle in his life. She kept cats though, by the hundred, I'd say—well, at least a dozen, and there were always half a dozen dogs. Big dogs. I asked what they were once, there's nothing like them around here. And she told me they were Irish Wolfhounds. She brought them in as pups and generation after generation they loped around the place, big as ponies.

Now, if you ever drive up to the Culley Place, the first thing you usually see, besides all those cats and the giant dogs, is Miss Culley herself, sitting on the porch, knitting or shelling peas, or doing one of the things that old women do on hot, dry summer days. But, no one was on the porch when I drove up and that gave me a bad feeling. Old folks die. And Miss Culley couldn't be less than a hundred by my reckoning.

I stopped the car and gave the horn a tap before me and Clover got out. Those big dogs perked up their ears, but they didn't look like they minded us about so I climbed down and hoisted Clover out behind me. Right away, Clover crinkled her nose up and let out a low growl. Warning growl's what I call it. She lifted her head twice like she was tasting the wind and hopped back in the cab. "Come on, Clov," I coaxed. But, she let out a huff like she was annoyed and edged back toward the window. I rolled down the window on my door. "Suit yourself," I said, "I reckon you'll come out quick enough if it gets hot." But, Clover lay down on the seat keeping one eye on the door of the Culley Place. I closed the door behind me and yelled out, "Miss Culley?" But, no one seemed to hear me but the dogs. One of them got up and padded over to give me a sniff and then lay back down.

I started up to the house and opened the screen door, but before I could give the door a big knock, it came flying open. I nearly tripped into the room I was so surprised. A tall girl was standing there in a yellow tee shirt and jeans. Her red hair was twisted up on top of her head and little strands of it fell around her face. She was wiping her hands on a dish towel and leaning on the doorframe impatiently.

"Well," she said, "What do you want?" sounding for all the world like Miss Culley.

I pulled my ball cap off real fast. "I was looking for Miss Culley," I said.

"Well, you found her," said the girl, flinging the dishtowel onto the sofa behind her, "I guess you'd better come on in."

I stepped inside the room, hat still in hand. "Actually," I said, "I was looking for Old Miss Culley."

"Oh," she said smiling, "Well, she's not about today. Maybe there's something I can help you with? I'm taking care of things while she's gone."

I looked around the room. It looked the same as I remembered. Drying herbs lined the ceiling on neat string lines. An afghan was thrown in the corner with two fat gray tabbies lounging on it. I could smell something sweet and full of vanilla baking in the other room.

Seeing my nose lift, she asked, "Want tea cakes? They're just coming out of the oven."

"I can't stay long," I said, "I've got my dog, Clover in the truck and it's a hot day."

49

"Wouldn't budge, would she?" she asked walking into the kitchen. I followed. She opened the over, an old cast-iron contraption, with use stains around the burners. "Well," she said, lifting the tea cakes out of the oven, "I reckon she'll come out if she gets hot enough. The other dogs don't mind."

"No," I said, "Miss Culley's dogs have always been friendly enough to strangers, dog or man."

She put the cookies down on the table after she had spread a dishtowel to shield the linoleum top. Using a big iron knife, she cut apart the cookies that had grown into one another. "So," she said, "What is it you came here for?"

I twisted my hat, "You'll think it's silly, a young girl like you'd probably laugh at country superstitions, but...well, a friend of mine said that Miss Culley helped him with a wolf problem."

The girl looked up eyes flashing, "Wolves, is it?" she said, "I suppose you want them killed."

"Not really," I said, "I don't mind them so much, only I want them to stop killing my sheep and move off; nothing else."

"Wolves kill sheep," she said flatly, "If I get them to move off your property, they'll only be hassling someone else. A wolf's got to eat, don't he?"

I nodded. "I reckon a wolf's got to eat same as anything else, but I'd rather he eat something besides my sheep."

She smiled. "Well, maybe I can do something about that after all." She put down the knife and slid the hot cookie tray into the sink. The sudsy water made a low hissing sound. "There's several things, actually, that might work," she said. She reached into a drawer and pulled out some dried herbs in small vacuum sealed bags. "If you have a little problem, you might want to use a deterrent, something like wolf's bane— aconite's its Latin name. They don't like the smell of it. You might tray scattering some of it dried, but it's better to grow it fresh. Course, that won't stop something hungry. That just stops a browser, someone interested in taking a look." She put the herbs down on the counter. "For hungry wolves, you need something strong, something fierce as they are." She squatted down and pulled open a low cabinet. There were several big jars all sealed with wax and labeled. She pulled out a big one with a clear yellow liquid in it. "This is from the zoo. A friend of mine gets it for me and I don't ask how. Smells something awful," she said wrinkling her nose.

"What is it?" I asked.

"Tiger pee," she said, "Nothing that a wolf hates more than a cat bigger than himself." "You might want to get yourself a dog too," she said. I opened my mouth to mention Clover, but she continued "A wolf dog, is what I mean. That dog in the car is fine for sheep herding and eating biscuits, but it takes a dog with a wolf's spirit to stand up to a pack."

"Well, there aren't many dogs like that around here," I said.

She smiled, "Well, maybe bring mine around and let them mark up the place. Briseis is expecting pups in a month or so. Maybe I could hold one for you."

I glanced back toward the door where I could see one of those big dogs peeking in through the screen. "Don't worry," the girl said laughing, "They don't bite—much!"

I frowned, "I was just wondering how Clover'd like a dog that big," I said.

"It won't start off so big," she said, "It'll have to work up to it." I nodded. "I'll bring them around first," she said, "See how the wolves like that, and we can see if your dog takes a liking to them. They're particular. They didn't like the smell of me much at first either, but they got used to me. A dog will even get used to wolves in time, and run with them."

I knew that. I'd seen wolf-dogs before. They were dangerous—as bold as any wolf without any fear of man. Like she was reading my mind she said, "Wolves weren't always afraid of men, you know. They had to learn it, just like anything will if it's hunted enough. You ever hear of the Seine?" she asked.

"Sin? Is that a place or something? I don't guess I have," I said.

"It's a river," she said, "In France. Big river. Probably nearly as big as the Mississippi, but it's nowhere as long. There was a time way back, in the 1300s when it froze through. Think of it. A river as big as the Mississippi frozen down to the core. Anyway, it froze and the wolves came across it right into Paris, right into the city. They weren't afraid then, you see. There were more wolves than men after the plague, and the wolves didn't have much to fear. But, they learned it later, when guns came and more and more men were born and less and less wolves. They remember, you see. They remember. Dog's memories aren't so long." I thought of Clover and the way she always jumped when the vent came on in the truck, even though she must've had that cool air hit her hundreds of times.

"Wolves remember," she said again, "That's why this," she said tapping the yellow jar, "and my dogs work so good. If the wolves get scared off once, they're likely to stay away unless a great need presses them." She looked out the window. The sun was failing and falling golden over the wooden floor. "It's not so bad here," she said. "There's plenty to eat besides sheep. It just takes a bit of work—for a wolf." She picked up the jar and pushes it and the bag of herbs into my hand. "You're dog'll be ready to go now. I'll bring my boys by in a week or so. See what we can do and check for tracks and marks to see how big a pack you have a problem with."

I nodded at her, my hands being full, "I'd be much obliged," I said.

She walked with me to the front door and pushed open the screen. "Don't be a stranger," she yelled after me. Clover barked once at her yell, and then slunk down in the seat. I carefully centered the jar and the herbs between me and Clover. She gave the herbs a sniff and then laid her head on her paws. I started up the truck and turned around careful of cats and big dogs and turned back down the dusty road toward home.

Well, Clover and I had an uneventful enough ride home and after a few days the girl showed up with those dogs, just like she said. I hadn't had a chance to try out any of her remedies yet and she said that was lucky enough since they would've spooked her dogs. It was already starting to get dark when she drove up and by the time she got all those big dogs out of the back of her truck and set them loping about, it was near to sunset. I studied the sky.

"Clear enough, I guess," she said, "We shouldn't have any problem with the weather."

I nodded. "You sure you want to be going out this late?" I asked.

"It's the reason I'm here," she said, "I didn't figure that wolves would come marching across your fields at mid-day." She whistled and those big dogs perked up their ears. "Reckon we'll take a look around and see what we see," she said. Then, she turned heel and headed off with her dogs toward the low pasture. I watched her 'til she was too small to make out clearly, and then clucked at Clover the come inside. She lingered a bit, her brown eyes watching the other dogs in the distance and then followed me. The screen door swung shut behind us and I pulled the heavy wood door closed for the night.

Now, the girl had said that she'd come back in the morning, but I still couldn't sleep. Dogs or not, it didn't seem right for her to be out there, just a girl, in the night. But, what could I do? She didn't even so much as take a rifle with her, not that I saw anyway. Big dogs or not, there are plenty of things prowling about in the night and wolves are the least of them. Mountain lions and rabid foxes and trigger-happy hunters with poor eyesight just to name a few. It might not be hunting season but that didn't stop some folks from getting off a shot or two at a deer. And, I remembered last year a bunch of boys had gotten liquored up and shot old Earl's best heifer thinking she was a prize buck. Some folks got more time than sense, I'd say. The feeling grew on me. Clover sat by the door and waited. Every now and then she thump her tail and it would make a dry whack on the wood floor. "Think I should go on out?" I asked her, "Make sure everything is okay?" Clover looked at me and gave her tail another whack. "I reckon you're right," I said.

I rummaged around in the cabinets 'til I found a flashlight with some juice left in it. I flicked it on and off and it gave out a strong steady light. Then, I took down my 30/30, the one with the sight and shoulder strap. Too bad my night eyes weren't what they were once. Still, it was a full moon, hunter's moon, and I thought I could hit a wolf if it came to it. For good measure, I jammed the herbs, wolfsbane she called it, in the pocket of my coveralls. I patted to make sure that I had everything—extra bullets, wolfsbane, pack of cigarettes, lighter. I grabbed a Moonpie, too. No sense in starving. Clover jumped up when I unlocked the door, wagging her tail something fierce. "No, girl," I said, "This isn't a night for you." She slumped down on the floor and put her head on her paws, looking at me dog-eyed. I reached down and scruffed the fur on her head, "I'll be back soon enough," I said.

I stopped on the porch to let my eyes adjust to the night. It was bright. That big full moon hung heavy and orange in the sky. I wasn't really sure which way to go, but after some thought, I started out the way I'd seen her go, over the low pasture toward the grazing fields. Once I crossed over the hill, the house was lost from sight. Clover must still be waiting by the door, I thought, hoping I'll come back for her. I walked a bit further. The air was crisp and colder than usually for a summer night. And, there was something else. Something like danger on the wind. Like a hint of electricity. A hunter'd know what I mean—it's that excitement you get right before a big buck comes into you line of sight. It's like you can feel him there before you can ever see him. I could see the sheep up ahead clustered together like a cloud gone to ground. They stirred a little when they smelled me, and milled in my direction expecting food or comfort. I knew they felt it, too. I had a sheep stung by a bee once come and duck its head under my arm. It's like the whole flock wanted to tuck themselves under and hide. You could smell something wild—that raw, sharp smell—I knew it through and through. All wild things have it, even stray cats and dogs. When wild cats broke into my barn and laid up in the straw, I knew it just by the smell. But, this was a little different. There was no smell of fear underneath. This smell was tangy and high and I knew just from the hint of it that it was old and didn't give a flip about me or any man.

The sheep gave a little collective shiver and pushed in on themselves. Then I saw one of those big dogs on sitting on the hill, like it was watching over the flock. I craned my eyes around and sure enough they were stationed all around, almost hidden front sight. Every dark eye fixed on the sheep, ready to pull down anything that didn't belong. I raised my hand, hoping they could see it was me, but the dogs didn't budge. These were professional dogs. They didn't give any little yips of acknowledgement like Clover and cock their ears. I was the same as the sheep to them. I walked through the flock and up past one of the dogs. He turned his eyes toward me, but didn't move, so I walked on into the night.

Now, it might seem strange that I didn't call out for the girl. But, to tell the truth, I didn't know her proper name. It was dark and clear and the moon hung low and full. Every tree, every blade of grass seemed outlined in light. There was just the slightest mist, a clash of the humidity earlier in the day and the coolness of this night, hanging low to the ground. I almost missed them—in the mist—low to the ground as they were. I crouched down on the hill sure they had seen me, but not a one moved. They sat in a circle, some on haunches and some laid down with head on paws like Clover was prone to do. There was a big wolf, gray and a half-head bigger than the rest, in the center and another wolf, dark, almost black, but slightly smaller facing him.

They weren't fighting, just staring nose to nose, like they were in the middle of something. A meeting of the minds, or the muzzles, at least, so it seemed. I felt a brush against my back and looked back to find myself eye to eye with one of those wolfhounds. He growled low in his throat. Warning growl. But, I reckoned he was warning me off or telling me to be careful. There are some things, maybe, a man isn't supposed to see. Just like there are something's that maybe a dog shouldn't get used to. I slunk back down the hill and walked back to the house. Clover was waiting for me at the door. I knew the big dog had followed me, though I never saw him. Clover gave a low growl and then a yip of recognition. I unlatched the screen door and stepped inside, leaning my rifle against the wall. I was getting old. The air seemed colder somehow and I was tired.

I don't know how long I sat there with Clover at my feet. I closed my eyes and laid my head against the back of the wooden chair. After some time, I heard the screen door open and felt Clover bristle against my leg. A low rumbling growl rippled through her body and I looked down to see her on her feet, fur raised. "It's all right, girl," I said, Clover growled again and kept to her feet.

"Guess it's hard to put up with," the girl said, standing at the door. Her red hair looked dark and there were bits of weeds caught in its tangled mass.

"Clover's not used to strangers," I said, patting the still bristling dog on the head.

"Those wolves won't be bothering you anymore," she said.

I nodded. "Plenty of room around here for wolves," I said, "I reckon they'll do just fine without my sheep."

She sniffed the air. "Could be a hard winter, though," she said, "Could be they'll come back if they have to."

I nodded again. "If the winter's hard, I reckon I could leave something out for them, to tide them over."

"That might do," she said, "I'll bring that pup around, when it's big enough." She turned and put her hand on the door.

"I won't forget what you've done for me," I said, "I'll return the favor if I can."

She turned back and smiled, her teeth glowing softly in the dark room, "I'll remember," she said. She opened the door and was gone. I saw two big dogs melt out of the dark and catch up with her. I watched her 'til she was gone from sight. Only when she had disappeared over the hill did Clover settled down by my feet. Men may be fooled by disguises, but no self-respecting dog ever will. I got up from the chair, careful to step over Clover, and locked the door. "It's getting late for us, Clover," I said. The dog stretched and gave one happy little yip, glad to be in her home on a crisp summer night.

Chapter 12:
Bramble Brew

Throughout my childhood we kept pigs. Our neighbors had pigs and most of the folks in the country had pigs of one sort or the other. Keeping pigs meant (usually) no more than five or six. But there were always a few farmers that kept more than that, and one of those lived right down the road from us. His pigs, hogs being a more accurate description, were notorious for escaping. They did not take well to having their liberty infringed upon once they were out and about. And the worst of the lot was Bramble Brew.

There are some people that will try to convince you that pigs are your friends. We certainly had several pigs in Critter Encounters at the Zoo and not only were they amiable, but they would gladly eat grain from your hand. The fact that they also ate zoo pamphlets and children's barrettes (sometimes snatched from the heads of unsuspecting toddlers) was unfortunate, but only increased their appeal. They were characters! Oh, those pigs. Such mischief makers! Those were the pigs in Critter Encounters, little pink swag-bellied concoctions that snuffled and snorted at the visitors.

But in another part of the Zoo were the Hogs. They weren't cute or fuzzy. They were black and had wiry razor-like tufts of fur. Their eyes were tiny and, well, piggy, and their teeth were very, very sharp. You didn't feed the Hogs handfuls of treats. You fed them wearing protective gloves and boots and quickly before their little piggy eyes turned your way. On gray days, their eyes glowed red I tell you! I swear. It's true. And, you could just see the thoughts buzzing behind their eyes. Thoughts of biting and gouging. Probably thoughts that focused around me. When they slept during the heat of the day, you could practically see the dreams twitching behind their little hog-eyes. And I can assure you that those dreams weren't pleasant.

Despite what you might've heard, hogs won't eat anything. They aren't dirty. And, they aren't slow-witted. They roll in mud to keep cool, but they are, otherwise, remarkably clean. And they are quite smart. Hogs remember. They remember that gates are sometimes left open by distracted girls that have too much to do. They remember that the gate has to be latched just so or a clever pig can lean against it and wait for that tiny "pop" that means now the pigs are free to run amok. Yes, pigs are very clever indeed. They have the patience of Job. And in the back of every pig's mind, even the pink and cuddly variety, is the primal memory of the Wild—of the feral hogs that roamed free and did whatever they pleased. Those hogs were not your friends. They didn't have friends. And they didn't want them.

Now, Bramble Brew was a Rhode Island Red. In her youth, she had won a prize at a County Fair (just like the infamous Wilbur and later "Babe.") But, in the long years from piglet to sow, Bramble Brew had lost any edge of cuteness. She was huge and formidable. Watching her move was like watching the slow yaw of a battleship. She gave the impression of slowness and inevitability. She did not so much move, as sail. But her slow and graceful gait belied her hidden speed. If roused, Bramble Brew could cover a field in a minute flat.

Nothing made Bramble Brew fiercer than having her liberties denied. Apples were hers by right. Piglets scattered when she crossed the hog-yard and grown dogs were known to cower when she let loose one of her angry squeals. Half-grown hogs dare not cross her shadow and should she escape her pen, it was near impossible to return her to it. After running amok for a day or a week, usually after all the sour apples and wild cherries had been eaten, the mud had dried up, and life outside the pen had soured, Bramble Brew would make her way home and wait outside the pen. It was best to let her in quickly and not ask questions. The other hogs averted their eyes. Bramble Brew was a force to be reckoned with and neither man nor hog had a right to question her.

But hogs don't live forever, even those as fierce as Bramble Brew. Most pigs live around a decade, but Bramble Brew lived twice that number and reached a mass of nearly a ton. And she died, as she lived, on her own terms. The night before she died, Bramble Brew burst out of her pen splitting through the low rails with the fury of a much younger hog and trotted down to the orchard. She spent the night gorging herself on withered autumn apples, wind-fall peaches, and persimmons and then fell into a deep sleep from which she never woke. The orchard had always been a favorite of Bramble Brew's and perhaps she wanted to see it one last time.

Bramble Brew died near twenty years ago, but if you visit the orchard in autumn in the evening when the shadows are heavy and the bees and hornets have gone to ground, you can still hear her snuffling for apples. And if you approach her favorite tree, the big one with the twisted trunk that looks more a crab apple tree than proper fruit tree, you're likely to hear a high squeal and if you do, you'd best run. Bramble Brew is no more willing to share apples in death than she was in life.

Chapter 13:
Curdled Milk

Mary was one of those girls with flawless skin and good eyes that everyone thought was pretty. She had a certain clear, clean look about her that passed for sweetness and while her beauty held, everyone believed she was just what they saw—a nice, sweet-faced girl with straw-colored hair. But Mary wasn't nice at all—she was selfish and vain. She never looked beyond her own mirror and never noticed the world around her unless she wanted something from it. She certainly never gave anything to anyone without expecting to get handfuls back. She was careless and rude and spilt things without wiping them up. Mary never did her own laundry; she had her sisters to do that for her. She never scrubbed pots with lye and ash to get them clean, since it would ruin her hands. She couldn't be bothered to help when jam was being made, since the steam gave her headaches. Mary sailed through life combing her hair and studying the fine lines of her hands. She liked to dip her feet into the coolest water in the stream and toss dandelions into the current. She thought that she could get by with her looks forever—and she might have it they had held.

But Mary was one of those girls who blooms early and whose looks are already faded by seventeen. Her bright hair, turned brown. Her blue eyes turned murky and her complexion, once compared to peaches and honey, became blotched and freckled. Her figure, always robust, started to grow pudgy. The only piece of beauty left to Mary by her eighteenth birthday was her hands—whose beauty she had always admired.

Suddenly, no one turned back to look at Mary when she passed. Her sisters no longer volunteered to do her chores. And, people complained at her laziness and rudeness. Faults that would've gone unnoticed years before were suddenly brought to Mary's attention. Mary had to start paying attention to things. She had to learn to hide her faults. But, stealth came easily to Mary. She found that she could lie without the least effort. She knew just what to say to get someone to look the other way—or to cast suspicion on another party. All those years of being beautiful and admired had taught Mary to be selfish and cruel. Now, she used her lies to get the things that she had once gotten with a look and a smile. It was harder work, but it was worth it.

By the time she was twenty, Mary was probably the biggest liar in the county, although no one knew it. She'd lie about the weather or the time of the day for the very spite of it. She lied about where she had been and what she had done— even if she had just been down to the creek to wash clothes or to pick flowers. She lied constantly and to everyone— including herself.

Not surprisingly, Mary's lies finally caught up with her, as lies have a way of doing. She found herself in a great deal of trouble—the kind of trouble that lies can only delay for so long. One bright summer day, Mary knew that she was going to have a baby. Some women might have been happy, especially those as lonely and friendless as Mary. But Mary was a selfish girl with a cruel streak and instead of thinking of her child, Mary thought, once again, only of herself. She contrived to hide the growing baby inside her with the thought of getting rid of the child once it was born. And that's just what she did.

Somehow, Mary managed to hide her growing middle and shortening hemline from everyone around her. It mightn't have been too difficult for such a sullen girl, a girl with no friends, who people avoided for her many lies. And, Mary managed it quite well. She had her baby alone, under a dark moon. And as she looked into its tiny bright eyes under that moon where another woman might've relented and thought of something other than herself, Mary looked at her child instead and contrived murder. She wrapped the baby tight in her shawl—as tight as she could—tight enough to hide its unhappy and surprised cries—and hid the baby in the wall in her bedroom. Then, she sealed the wall with mud and paper and curled back up in her bed and sleep through the night.

But even if Mary had no heart at all, her child certainly did. He had a heart full of righteous anger at the injustice done to him and he wasn't about to let Mary get away with her deceit. Every night, tiny fingers scratched on the wall beside Mary's bed and cries could be heard coming from the wall. Sometimes only Mary heard the cries. She could be sitting at the kitchen table and while the rest of her family heard only bird's singing and the rush of the creek's waters, Mary heard the small accusing cry of her son.

After a while, her face grew haggard and white. She pulled at her hair 'til it came out in clumps. She often stopped in the road and looked back at the cabin questioningly, as if she heard something that no one else could hear. After a year, Mary threw herself in the river. She was found floating down stream, her hands still clasped on her ears, a look of utter guilt locked on her face.

You would think that Mary's death would be the end of this story, but it seemed not to be. Mary's old cabin got the reputation of being haunted—not by Mary herself—though some whispered that she was the cause of it—but by a small ghostly child. People often heard the patter of small feet on the cabin's wooden floors. Scratching was heard in the walls and a small misty image was often seen near the cabin picking flowers or running in play. People who rode by the cabin often saw the small figure—too hazy to be made out clearly— running by the side of their wagons or horses. Some said it looked like a puppy and others like a child of three or four. And although no one could ever remember the figure doing anything troublesome, the cabin got a reputation. It gave folks an uneasy feeling just walking or riding by it, and, after a while, no one would dare think of living in it.

It was, in its own way, unheard of—a perfectly good cabin with a nice garden plot and stables just sitting empty. People rented the cabin. A family or two even bought it for a few months or even a year, but as sure as rain they'd be gone in no time flat complaining of they knew not what: an odd feeling, an unrightness, a strange melancholy that would seize a body with no warning. At first, they tried to convince themselves that it was something else—certainly not a ghost. It was unstable ground, maybe the cabin was built over a cave or a hidden sink-hole. Maybe the strange whimpering noise they heard was the wind in the eaves. Surely that scampering sound was squirrels on the roof or mice in the walls or under the floor-boards. Any white figure glimpsed was a stray cat or a neighborhood dog. What else could it be? What else would it be?

But, the one thing they couldn't reconcile, the one thing that no amount of explanations could factor was the spoiled milk. No milk could stand in that cabin not for a day, not for an hour. You could milk your cow in the stable and walk with a fresh pail to the house only to find it curdled at the front door. A glass of milk drank in the front yard would be fine, but on the porch or the front room it would sour immediately. Milk left to sit gave off the distinct scent of regret and sorrow. It was the mystery of the milk, more than anything else that drove the people out.

After a few years, no one thought of living in the cabin. The roof grew slanted and the shutters knocked during storms. The once carefully tended garden went to seed and the stables lost boards in storms that were never replaced. After twenty years, the house was barely standing and the stable had fallen in a dry heap. The garden had gone wild and garlic and Joe Pye Weed grew in tangled masses with day lilies and Sweet William. The house stood lonely and since no one ever bothered to pass it, no one knew if the tiny white figure still played in the lanes or waited for a passerby.

So, everyone was surprised when someone finally bought the house. No one even knew it had been for sale. Over time, people on the Creek had come to think of the house in the terms of an abandoned barn or a Widow Maker Tree—a part of the landscape best to be avoided, but as permanent a fixture as the air and the sky. It was a shock to us all to see a blue Prius parked in the dirt driveway, glutted as it was by weeds. It was more of a shock to hear that the cabin was being refurbished— brought back to life as it were.

"No one stays there long," we all muttered, "They'll be gone by the time the first leave falls." But, the new owners weren't gone by autumn. They came in the day and worked on the house and left at night. They came with builders and surveyors and fresh wood with "Lowe's" stamped on it in blue. They came with new shingles and flowers set neatly in six-and nine-pack containers. They came to stay.

Now, these people, the Smith-Stansons, came from the City. And they had heard all their lives, no doubt feed by reruns of The Andy Griffith Show and Green Acres, that country people were friendly. This is, of course, not strictly true. Some country people may be friendly. Some might on occasion bring you a pie or freshly baked bread on your first moving day. Some might wave from the side of the road at a stranger driving by. And some might even stop by to tell you that the kind of grass your installing in your front yard plug by plug won't "set 'round here." But country people are also suspicious.

Strangers or city folk are viewed with humor at best and disdain at worst. They won't last the winter, they don't plant things with no regard for the earth, they have too many gadgets and no respect for the way things are done, and worst of all, they're meddlesome. City folks, again fed by a thousand movies peopled with waving, straw-chewing yokels, will run you down in your field to ask you questions that any fool would know the answer to. They stop you when you're rounding up your stray cows that broke through the rear-pasture fence and have gotten themselves a mile or two down the road to ask if you're taking them for a walk. Sometimes they want to take a picture. They ask what kind of cows you have, what kind of dog, what style of architecture was used for your barn-design. In short, they have no sense at all.

The Smith-Stansons were viewed with amusement and caution. They sure had a lot of builders working on their house. They should've known that no one could live in that house. They could've asked anyone. Of course, if they had, people would've told them just that—no one lives in that cabin for long. No one would've told them why—no one would've mentioned ghosts, haints, apparitions or anything of the like. It was understood when you said no one lived somewhere that there was a reason why and it wasn't due to geological disturbances or bad insulation. But, the Smith-Stansons, even if they had been told, wouldn't have believed what they were hearing. They believed in science, the large cable network dish that they installed, and Lowe's Home Improvement Warehouse. In their opinion, there was nothing ingenuity and a credit card couldn't solve. They complained that there were no cell phone towers and that they had to install a conventional phone. They wondered that no one else seemed to care or even have cell phone. If they heard a strange noise in their walls the first week or found things strangely misplaced after they returned from a trip to the mall, they didn't seem to notice. Everything was still hectic anyway—boxes lay unpacked in the main room, spare shingles were still waiting to be put in the newly constructed garage, and plants, still in the quart buckets, sat in a row awaiting their chance to grow in the true earth. But, then there was the spoiled milk.

Sarah Smith-Stanton soon found that no milk could be kept in the house. It didn't matter if it was refrigerated and two weeks from its expiration date. You could freeze it, pack it in ice, or leave it out on the table. It didn't matter one whit. Milk brought into the house fresh from the grocery store and opened standing at the sink counter would curdle while you poured it in a glass. The cat was in a tizzy, and, frankly so was Sarah. No amount of science, television, or self-help books could explain away all that spoiled milk. It began to worry Sarah, in the small niggling way that things do that you push to the back of your mind, but you just can't forget.

It was something to do with the thermostat, she told herself. Or, it was just a bad run of milk—the grocery stores in this area were very unreliable. It was the tilt of the house, the angle of the sun, or forgetfulness on her part. But, no matter how many times that Sarah told herself that it was nothing, that it was unimportant, that it was only a carton of milk, the more she can to realize that the carton of milk, that all the cartons of milk were only a symptom and not the problem at all. And the cat, in his own self-satisfied way, agreed completely. Spoiled milk was a huge problem for him. This was his house, and by proxy, his milk. Something would have to be done.

For two weeks straight the cat begged for milk. He pulled out all the stops. He tried the big eyes, the gentle kneading, the twinning around the legs. He then tried tipping over his water, shredding the tablecloth, and bringing in mice with more than a little life still left in them. But his owners had stopped buying milk. The cat was perplexed. It was lucky that he had neighbors so nearby. Neighbors with kitchens. Neighbors with cows. Nice kind neighbors that would take pity on a poor underfed cat. But although the cat found milk readily enough from neighbors and other cats' dishes, he was not appeased. This was his house. And it was his milk. Something would have to be done.

Now, the cat, being a cat, was quite aware of the small smudgy white spirit that lived in the house and the gardens. It never bothered the cat, since, being a cat, he saw many things that people didn't. People, he mused, who were so good at opening cans and pouring milk, were little good at the most basic of things—such as seeing what was there to be seen or hearing the most obvious of noises.

The ghost, for his part, was also aware of the cat. There had been other cats in and around the house over the years. Small animals, raccoons, mice, 'possums, and foxes, had lived under the house and in the garden for years. But these creatures, who stared mildly at the little ghost or ignored him depending on their nature, were nothing like the cat. The cat was interested. He was interested the way a cat will be when another cat is drinking his milk or sitting on his cushion. The cat, with the sharp and piercing hate of any cat, cut right to the root of the problem. The ghost had to go. It was the cause of "NO MILK." No milk was a problem in the cat's book. A big problem. And, the cat meant to take care of it. One way or the other.

But the cat ran into a bit of trouble. The ghost, unlike another cat or a neighbor's meddlesome Pekinese, couldn't be chased off. The ghost didn't seem to mind the cat's hissing, growling, chasing, or biting. The ghost, in fact, could not be bitten or scratched. And when the cat tried, the ghost just laughed. This was very annoying to the cat. Even more annoying was the fact that Sarah, his owner, had taken him to the Vet twice saying that the cat was suffering from some sort of nervous condition. The Vet administered some horrible ear-drops that made the cat feel sleepy and slightly off-balance. After that, the cat was very careful not to menace the ghost around Sarah. This was to be guerilla warfare. And the cat was certain that if there was to be a winner, then that winner would wear whiskers.

But the cat's attempts at covert action met with no more success than did his previous direct attacks. The ghost could not be frightened or even surprised. The ghost seemed to know just where the cat was hiding even when he crawled under the porch and lay still as old leaves or crawled under a quilt peering out the afghan holes. The ghost knew and then he laughed. It was the laughing that gave the cat pause. A laughing enemy is a dreadful thing, and, well, if you can't beat an enemy, then there's only one real course of action.

One thing that every feline knows as well as his whiskers and the swish of his tail is that it's better to join forces with an enemy than to lose right out. Cats don't like losing, and this cat was no exception. But making friends is hard on a cat and the ghost was immune to his usual manipulations. The ghost wasn't interested in purrs and happy little mews. And when the cat tried to lean on the ghost, he fell right through. No, the only thing the ghost seemed interest in was milk. But there was no milk to be had. Not for ghosts and not for cat.

Not one to give up lightly, the cat had a plan. He had observed, on occasion, that the Stanton-Smiths added milk that was not-milk to their coffee. To his mind, this was a waste of perfectly good milk, even if it wasn't really milk at all. It had a strange heavy smell that reminded the cat of the thing they called butter. It was close to milk, he supposed, and after observing the pouring of the not-milk for a few days, he decided it would have to do.

The not-milk that Cat learned was called "Pass me the cream," was usually kept in the refrigerator except of morning when it lived on the table near the foul steaming cups of coffee. Cat had tasted coffee once and once was all he cared to taste it. Why not-milk should be wasted in such a fashion was a mystery to Cat, but then humans were strange creatures. It was Cat's opinion that their motives were best left unanalyzed.

Sunday was the day that the not-milk was left out the longest. It was a day of long mornings and newspapers and much pouring of coffee. Sometimes there were pancakes and sometimes the not-milk was left out on the table along with muffins, jam, and other things the cat liked to touch with his paw (and sometimes lick) when there was no one to stop him.

Cat had observed that things were more likely to be left out in the open if there was no cat present. So all Sunday morning he hit himself under the pie-safe peering into the kitchen until the Stanton-Smiths had drank their share of foul-smelling coffee, eaten their muffins, and decided to go on a constitutional. The ghost, the cat noted, was also bidding his time. He too liked to observe things from a distance. Although the Stanton-Smiths seemed unaware of his presence, the cat could clearly see the ghost behind the broom—fuzzy and insubstantial, but there nonetheless.

After the Stanton-Smiths left, Cat jumped on the table. He walked around the plates and stuck a paw in some blackberry jam. He did not care for it. Then he lowered his head and began to push the small carton of cream to the edge of the table. When it was at the very edge, he looked at the ghost and mewed and then he pushed. The cream container landed on the floor and immediately began to ooze not-milk. Soon there was a substantial puddle on the floor. Cat had to admit that it looked and smelled very inviting, but it wasn't for him. He mewed again, his plaintive best, and then he looked at the ghost.

The ghost moved toward the cream and sat looking at it for a very long time. It looked at the cat and then the cream and then at the cat again. Then the ghost laughed and made a very small sigh. There was the smallest flash like a light bulb makes right before it goes dim, and then milk was gone and so was the ghost. And he stayed gone and the milk stayed fresh and the cat was happy there for many years.

Eventually, the Stanton-Smiths moved to another house and cat along with them. And other families and cats and dogs and even parakeets came to live in the cabin. But the ghost never returned and the cabin was quiet.

Of course, you can never really know what happens to a ghost, why a haunting stops, or if it really even has. But I do know that my childhood was filled with stories about the Milburne cabin. We'd dare each other to go up to the front door when we were kids and listen for the baby in the walls. The cabin was unoccupied until around fifteen years ago when a family came in and refurbished it. They had an especially large orange Tom cat that liked to sit on the front porch and smirk and people walking on the road. After they moved in, there weren't any more stories about the ghost and the lady that lives in the cabin these days says it's as peaceful a house as you could hope for. Having cats of my own and knowing how clever they are, it seems likely that the arrival of the cat and the departure of the ghost was no mere coincidence.

Chapter 14:
Dark Earth

Anyone who works in the soil, whether it's a full-blown farm or a patch of dirt that can boast a few veggies or perennials, knows earth has a soul of its own. It changes with the seasons. It has its own moods. Sometimes things sprout up just fine with minimal care; sometimes you get brambles and weeds. The earth has a long memory. Just about every patch of it has probably been someone or something's grave in the long history of the planet. We walk and live and grow on soil that has echoes. And there are some patches of this earth where the echoes are ever so dark and the shadows very long.

There are some people who would have you believe that farming is a science. That success or failure depends solely on acidity levels, rainfall per annum, and the correct amount of fertilizer. And, no doubt, all their theories are true. Science will fatten your cattle and grow your corn high. It will rid you of Japanese beetles and dust the aphids from your roses. But science has no inkling of the darkness of the Earth, just as it fails to comprehend the mysteries of a man's heart.

Country people know that the Earth is a mystery and farming an art as mysterious and primal as the Earth itself. Every farmer knows that even driving his new tractor with the green paint still gleaming from the factory, he is only a heart's breath away from a shaman shaking his stick at the sun and moon. The Earth is not to be reckoned with—there's no way around her. The Earth will have things her way and the sooner you come to accept that fact, the better. You can fertilize, introduce lady bugs and mantis, spray pesticides, irrigate, and test the soil with regularity, but no man can influence the pull of the moon, the tilt of the Earth, or the change of the seasons.

No man can predict with complete certainty if a winter will be wet or dry or if the rain with nurture or flood your soil.

In the country, you follow the signs: the size of new oak leaves, the color of a wooly worm, the coming of the first frost of the spring rains. But even the signs can fail you, or worse, be nothing more than a trick—like so many shadows in the darkest parts of the wood. The Earth is fickle, and often cruel. She's full of tricks and she's never forgiven anyone or forgotten anything. Deep within her core are stored all men's hopes and dreams, as well as their lies and deceits. And, ever so often, she dredges one of a dozen up to the surface for all the world to see. What are floods, famines, and droughts, but the worst of men's fears and evils? What are rainbows and spring snows that melt as the fall other than the lightest of our hopes made flesh?

I never realized the power of the Earth or the pull that she had on me until I left the country. I grew up in the country on a small farm. We had a garden, cows, a trio of fat horses, ten sullen pigs, and a gaggle of chickens that were supposed to lay their eggs in the hen-house's neat boxes, but more often than not laid them under bushes or in the ditches. The cows were prone to chasing children and small dogs, as were the chickens and their evil cousins, the speckled guineas. The horses refused to be ridden. They were plow horses, and, as such, were much too proud for any nonsense. The pigs loved anyone with a pail in hand, but were possessed with a great hatred for anyone that dared disturb them without producing a handout of sour mush or even apples in a pinch. There were dogs and cats on our farm as well. A respectable assortment of pets that earned their keep and wouldn't dream of wearing rhinestone studded collars. Most of them would've died of embarrassment if a doggy sweater or a Christmas hat had been presented to them.

The cats patrolled the corn crib with a regularity that most drill sergeants would have admired. Mice and corn snakes were an enemy they were bred to hate and even the tiniest kitten, his eyes open only a week, would hiss and spit at the mere mention of a mouse. The dogs were shepherds and hounds, for the most part—a sturdy mixture of country blood that could be traced back to the black and white dogs that travelled over land from Virginia with the first of my family. These dogs, well aware of their long and illustrious heritage, herded and hunted and kept the motley assortment of "critters" off of our property.

Critters came in a variety of pestersome forms. There were the small brown mice and large snakes that liked to curl up in the corn crib. There were raccoons and 'possums—both notorious thieves with a cunning that most super-villains would covet. There were foxes who would steal a unsuspecting chicken right off her perch or snatch a duck out of pen before you could blink you eye, as well as fat black snakes that swallowed eggs, and often chicks, whole. Sometimes there were coyotes, with their dog-like faces and almost-human eyes. All together, the country is a dangerous place for anything small or feathered. Chicken, ducks, geese, and even calves have only luck and the presence of a stout dog between them and all the marauders the forest can produce.

Then, there were the moles. Their benign, velvety appearance belied the total annihilation they were capable of wrecking on a garden or a yard. In their absent-minded way, they dug swaths of destruction across fields and produced weak foot-falls that could easily cost a horse or cow a broken leg. Moles were the specialty of my cat, Licorice. For days, she would lay in wait for a mole. Watching from a stone or a tree overlooking the garden, she would map the brown intruder's movements. Then, after observing her enemy and his proximity to the surface, she would make her move. One quick pounce was usually enough to end the mole's oblivious career. One summer, later called The Summer of the Moles, Licorice systematically killed twenty-three moles. Each day for nearly a month, she would lay one small mole body on the porch at dawn. She had found their burrow, and, in her cat-like cruelty, decided to stretch out the mole's destruction. Later, I would think about those moles, waiting in their den for Licorice to come each morning—unable, in their mole-ish torpor, to escape.

Now, it's my belief that you could drop two farmers from any place, or for that matter anytime, together, and once they got of the difficulty of the language barrier, they'd get along just fine. First they'd discuss how bad the weather had been, and how bad it was likely to be in the future. One would ask the other what he was growing. And if the fellow was cultivating something different than himself he would express some surprise and ask how the other fellow got along with such a crop. The other farmer would, of course, say not so well as one might hope, but enough to get by and both would nod. Farmers, as a rule, are pessimists always expecting the worst, but seldom getting it. Mother Nature may be a cruel mistress, but she tends to look on the bright side with a hope of spring and light rains in the future. Farmers do not and perhaps with good reason. There is always spring as sure as there is winter. There are also droughts, storms, and blights.

Blights are the hardest to understand even in the face of science. At the turn of the 20th century, the Chestnut tree was probably the most important food and timber tree in the country ranging in groves from Maine to Michigan, down through Indiana and Illinois, and south to Alabama and Mississippi, and then spreading eastward into the Appalachians. But in four decades, thirty million acres of Chestnut trees were gone—all taken by blight. A few groves were spared in remote places and scientists have been hard at work developing a hybrid Chestnut (so far with no luck) since the 1930s. But the American Chestnut that was the backbone of forests in the Southeast is a memory. In less than a man's lifetime, the Chestnuts died leaving only their bones. Chestnut wood, much like poplar, is resistant to rot and insects. You can still see split rail fences with Chestnut rails and there's a good chance to most cabins and houses with rock foundations built before the blight have either a Chestnut or Poplar base.

No one can predict blight. We've had blights of Hemlock, Magnolia, and Elm. But none with the intensity of the one that struck the Chestnut. They died silently and by the millions and maybe their spirits are still in the soil waiting for the perfect hybrid that will allow them to return. The earth remembers even when the men and squirrels and deer have forgotten the sweet, low taste of the American Chestnut and few can recall her high canopies and her particular grace, the earth remembers. Can there be ghosts of trees? The next time you're in the woods or even in your own backyard or favorite park, stop and listen. Can you hear it? Can you hear a low sad sigh on the wind? Maybe it was just the trees. Maybe it was just their ghosts.

Chapter 15:
Learning to Witch

You can't throw a rock in the country and not hit a witch of some kind. Mind, they don't call themselves witches—with the exception of water witches—and that's a long-held title of honor. But there are folk that can heal a sick calf, tell your fortune with coffee grounds, whistle up a rain, or tell you what to do if you'd like your neighbor to have a sudden urge to move to another climate. We don't put a label on these things. They're just as much a part of the South as hoe-cakes and sweet tea, and a part of what makes it such an interesting place.

My uncle was a water witch. It was an honorable calling, but not a fulltime position. Not a soul in the country would've thought of digging a well without a witch walking the place first. Even from the road side, he could tell if a field had the feel of water. I can remember us, my sister, cousins, uncle and father and me, walking by the new city neighbor's field and watching as the well-diggers plied their trade. "What do you think?" my dad asked my Uncle Vernon.

Vernon shook his head. "Nothing worth having," Vernon said kicking the ground, "Sulfur at best." My dad nodded. We knew about sulfur, even a witch couldn't always predict it. My uncle wiped the sweat off his brow with the back of hand. "I'd have to walk it to be sure," he finished. And we all walked on.

In a few days my dad told Zuzu and me that the city fellow's water was sulfur after all and it would have to be capped. This pleased everyone. "Should've called in a witch," my uncle said. Everyone agreed. "Things should be done right the first time," my dad said.

Now, my sister and I had developed a dread fascination with water witching. The chances of us having the talent were poor, we knew. First, most witches were men. No one could explain why, it just was. Second, the talent mostly passed down in a family direct and our father wasn't a water witch—and our mother surely didn't have a drop of witch in her blood. She dismissed water witching as nonsense, but then she was from the city and didn't know any better. The town she grew up in had a Dairy Queen and a drive-in movie. The thought of ice cream bought on the slightest whim was more than my sister and I could conceive. It took twenty minutes for us to bike to the country store for ice cream cups that had been sitting so long in the freezer they'd turned gummy around the edges. Not that we were complaining. Ice cream was ice cream and gummy edges could be picked off. But back to the matter of witching, we'd set our hearts on it and determined we would have lessons and after we'd pestered my uncle for a month, he agreed.

Now, water witching, as with any well-defined science, has its own proper tools and regulations. First, my uncle told us all to go find a good twig. Hazel or willow was best, but whatever twig took our fancy was fine as well. I choose a long twisty apple twig with a fork at the end. The fork was important. In the hands of a proper water witch, a twig would bend down at that fork and show where water was hidden. I thought I would give the twig a little help by bending it down a bit, but Zuzu saw me and said she would tell. My cousin Carley said it was cheating flat out, but I didn't listen to her since she cheated at just about everything from marbles to hopscotch.

As it turns out, my cousin, like her father, did have a talent for water-witching, which is rare in women in these parts. None of the rest of us ever had any luck, not with peach, willow, or hazel. There's an art to dowsing and maybe a bit of magic, too. And maybe that's what makes it so interesting. The country is a place of hidden things—foxfire, sinkholes, secret

78

caverns, and haints. Wampus cats cry out with the voice of children and lost spirits still roam the logging roads and forgotten byways. There is a darkness mingled with everything bright and an old magic that turns stories into legends and sticks into dowsing rods.

If you have a mind to dowse for water, it's easy enough to give it a try. Even Albert Einstein, that bastion of all things scientific, was a believer in it. It's easy enough to attempt - just find yourself a "Y" shaped stick. Different folks have different opinions on the best wood, but most agree that flexibility is key. Some people even swear by brass or metal, and I've heard of one fellow who uses a coat hanger shaped into a "Y." To each his own. The principle is easy enough—hold out the stick, think of water, and walk. The stick or hanger should tilt decidedly down when you find water. Of course, unless you find a creek, well, or lake, you may have to dig for confirmation. It's a useful skill should you want to dig a well and sure to dazzle your friends. You'll also be keeping an old tradition alive. Water-witching goes back 8,000 years—near as long as good storytelling.

Chapter 16:
Bred in the Bone

I've heard about mud men all my life. They're a sort of country golem, and I was surprised to learn that other folks weren't familiar with them. There are lots of stories about bringing up the dead or calling back in the South. Some of them deal with mud men. This story was inspired by those stories, as well as my love of a good mystery.

There were some folk that thought being the only source of law in a small town was light work. But Prosper Vance knew better. He'd been sheriff in Holbert Valley for going on twenty years and deputy for fifteen before that. If there was anything that confirmed your worst suspicions about human nature, Prosper reckoned, lawing was sure to do it. Generally, it was the little pieces of meanness that stuck most with you. Unchecked those petty hatreds and slights tended to grow like weeds and often ended up with someone's body found in an unmarked grave.

As Prosper stared down at Keefe McCalister's body, he thought it a small miracle that ole Keefe hadn't ended up in a hole sooner. Keefe wasn't, or more properly, hadn't been a bad man, but he hadn't been a good one either. It was common knowledge that it was Keefe who had done for Roan Everett only a month before. Keefe and Roan had a case of hate at first sight since grade school and had fought over whiskey, women, and cards since that time. There seldom a weekend since the two had hit puberty that one hadn't ended up hauled down to the jail or given a good talking to. Since Roan was shot by accident it would seem—if drunkenness and Russian roulette could be considered accidents—the town had been a whole heap quieter. And with Keefe lying six feet under it was likely to be quieter still.

It was, Prosper thought, a strange killing—though the victim was not unexpected. Keefe's face was unmarked, but his body was bashed and bludgeoned. It was caved in near-flat in places as if someone had been at him with a sledge hammer. Whoever had done for Keefe had a passionate hate going. And yet, the body, when it was found hidden high in the hills was cared for as if by kin. Wrapped in linen and laid reverently in the ground, there was even a rough cross on Keefe's breast. Almost as if two men, and not one, had a hand in it. True, Prosper knew, some murderers took to remorse after a killing, but those were most likely to confess and often killed with a heated heart.

Lovers done wrong often wept over their murders and begged forgiveness as they were hauled off to their fates. But in his long career, Prosper had yet to see a murder of this violence paired with such a respectful burying. It was perplexing and filled him with a strange dread. Any man who could behave in such a way and then turn civilized over a burial was touched by some sort of devil. There were, in this wide world, Prosper knew, such folk about—yet he had hoped never to encounter one in his jurisdiction.

It came to his mind, unbidden, that most folk would suspect Roan Everett's father—seeing as Keefe had killed his only son a month earlier. But Prosper had known Old Man Everett—as well as the man could be known—since he was himself a boy. And though it could not be argued that the Old Man was uncanny, he was not the type to turn to vengeance. Keefe had other enemies and friends that fought him of occasion who may've had cause to come at him with gun or knife. But this work was more than a moment of recklessness.

It was on these matters that Prosper was ruminating, sitting on his haunches and looking into the grave, when the County Examiner, Will Scott, pulled up in a battered ole Jeep that looked like an Army surplus repainted—which was what it was. "Had a hell of a time getting up here, Prosper," Will yelled up from the Jeep.

"Well, I don't think our killer was thinking of your convenience," Prosper said as he stood to full height.

Will walked over and peered down into the hole, "Son of a bitch!" he said, "What the hell did that?"

"Reckon that's the County Examiner's job to ascertain," Prosper said.

"Well," Will said, "I think my official first opinion will have to be 'damned if I know.' That's a piece of work, that is. Some sort of hammer or shovel, do you think?"

"Those strikes look bigger," Prosper said, "And rounder and deeper than a man could make with a hammer or spade."

Will began to open his bag and called back to his assistant still waiting by the Jeep. "He's a little jumpy," he said to Prosper, gesturing to the boy walking up the path, "Straight out of school and a murder his first week."

"Run of bad luck," Prosper said.

Will looked back down at the body. "For everyone concerned," he agreed.

Two days later, a second body turned up. This one laying at the edge of town crushed near flat. It took dental records and a good deal of cussing by Will Scott to identify the man as John Willum—a lay-about that came into town for a weekly game of dice. The killer took no pain to hide this kill or the next two that showed up. One a known moonshiner named Michaels, who folk generally liked, and the other a girl named Ann that lived down by the river with her grandmother. The dead had nothing in common but their fate and Prosper was hard pressed to think of a reason—other than pure malice—that anyone would've had to harm these particular three souls. Any man who knew Willum wasn't likely to be familiar with Ann, other than from a distance. She had been a pretty girl and was in training to be a teacher. It was known that Roan Everett had dated her while they were both back in school. But she had little to do with him in the year before his death. Besides, Roan was in the ground himself. The friends he had left behind—easily counted on one hand—were little likely to take revenge on an old love of his. That left only Roan's father, and there was no doubt that the man had been acting odd as of late.

Old Man Everett had asked that his son be buried up near his house instead of in the local bone yard. That hadn't been taken as strange, at the time, since folk had family cemeteries all over the Valley. But there was word that the Old Man had the boy dug up and moved elsewhere—though no one could say for sure. And folk that had seen Everett since Roan's death said he was strange-eyed and wild acting; not his usual self. But losing a son—especially an only son—can change a man, Prosper knew. Still, he thought it best if he spoke to the man, for it might be that he knew of some friend of Roan's that had taken the dead boy's scores upon himself.

Old Man Everett's house was big by Valley standards and sat high in the hills. A long elm-shaded path led to it and a fellow sitting on the house's long, low porch could see visitors coming from a mile or more away. When Prosper rounded the curve and caught his first glimpse of the dark-wooded structure, he could see that the old man was waiting on the porch and that another fellow was standing under the trees shading his eyes with his hand. But when he pulled up to the gravel lot and parked his car, the shaded man was gone and the old man was sitting by himself rocking.

"Mind if I come up for a while," Prosper called as walked up the path and when the old man nodded he climbed the porch stairs and sat.

"Thought you might be up," the old man said, "I heard about poor little Ann."

"She was friends with your son," Prosper said.

The old man laughed then, but there was no joy in it. "Not many was friends with my son," he said. "Ann was a girl with good sense and got shut of him quick enough."

"All men have their faults," Prosper said, "and I'd be the last to speak ill of the dead."

The old man nodded, "So would I. They say the dead listen to living folk from where they are. But some don't hold with such things. I haven't had much cause to speak to you, Sheriff Vance, but I wonder what you think about such matters."

"I think I saw a fellow there under those trees when I pulled up," Prosper said.

"Maybe there was," the old man said, "or maybe it was just them elms casting a shadow. In these hills you can't always tell what you see."

"Maybe that's so," Prosper said, "And maybe some friend of your son's believes that he has reason to feel wronged."

"I doubt," the old man said sadly, "That there are two or three even in this world that shed a tear for Roan." He turned and looked at Prosper dead on then and said, "I may've been his father, but I wasn't blind. You hope and you pray, but sometimes there's no changing things—least of all the heart of a man."

"If you knew something," Prosper said, "Something that would help me find the man that killed Ann and the others, you'd tell me."

The old man sighed and then began to rock, "If I knew something to be told, I'd tell you." He said, "But there are some things that walk in this world that your law has no hold over."

"Well," Prosper said, "I'd still like you to send me word if you hear of something—one way or the other."

The old man nodded and after a while, Prosper got up and left. As he drove down the hill, he could see the old man rocking still in his rear-view mirror and something dark and reddish that flirted through the shadows along the path. A deer, maybe, but a big one. Or maybe something else that he didn't want to imagine.

When Prosper got back to the jail, there was a message waiting for him from the County Examiner. There were pieces of clay embedded in the bodies, some lanced into their shattered bones. Will reckoned it might've been that the murder instrument—maybe some kind of farm tool—was dirt encrusted at the time that it was used. But the clay was the same in all instances and seemed to come from one source.

Another message asked him to stop by Hollister Hardware—there had been a break-in last night though nothing seemed taken—only a few windows shattered. The Hollister place was right on the edge of town and well-known for its weekly card game. It was also the place that Roan Everett had met his maker a month or more ago—bleeding out before an ambulance could make its way from the County Hospital. There was still a blood patch on the wood floor in the back room.

Folk said that the blood of a murdered man would never be washed off. But Prosper knew for a fact that blood soaked into wood would not be washed whether it came from a man or a critter. It was enzymes that kept the shadow of blood on the hardware store floor and not a vengeful haint. Still, Billy Hollister was in a near fit by the time Prosper pulled up to the hardware store. He took Prosper to the back room where the blood still looked new on the oak. He pointed, finger shaking in rage, at four broken windows and an unhinged door.

"Son of a bitch busted up the whole back of the store," Billy said.

"Don't reckon you saw who did this?" Prosper said.

"Sure I did," Billy said, "I was in the front closing up when the big heavy-footed bastard clean knocked the back off the store."

"You might've called last night," Prosper said.

"What good would it have done?" Billy said, "I had that twitchy little insurance fellow to deal with all morning. Reckon you could wait 'til after."

Prosper sighed, "Did you get a look at his face?" Prosper asked, "Did he look like any fellow you knew?"

"Oh, I knew him all right," Billy said, "Though I wouldn't rightly say you could call him a man."

"What the hell is that supposed to mean?" Prosper asked. "Either it was a man or it wasn't."

"Wasn't then," Billy said. "Wasn't anything that I ever saw before—but it was like a man and I can name the one."

Prosper tapped the table, "I know what you're going to say, Billy, for you've been saying it all about town this morning. And you know well as I do that Roan Everett is dead and buried."

Billy snorted, "I don't suppose that being either would stop him much."

"Well," Prosper said, "that puts me in a fine pickle—there's no law governing dead folk I reckon."

Billy nodded, "True enough. And doesn't that just put everything on his side."

"If you see anything again or anyone," Prosper said, "you be sure to let me know."

"I will," Billy said, "and if I see that bastard Roan Everett I'm going to put a hole in him—dead or not."

There were times that Prosper thought he had made a bad career decision the day he took up lawing. This was one of them and, of late, there had been quite a few. Folk were dead and it was easy enough to see who was behind the killings. The only problem being that the most likely suspect was dead himself. Folk were talking. They took to locking their doors and kept the curtains drawn by night. Though no one mentioned by name what they all knew to be true, they kept away from dark places and fortified themselves with crosses and charms and comforts against the darkness. Prosper was not a believer in such comforts, though he wasn't opposed to a stiff drink on a cold night—which was a comfort of its own.

Prosper considered himself a simple man—though, in truth, he was deep-minded and though slow to speak, he said a lot. He had seen just about all the wickedness man had to offer, as well as a surprising amount of good. Roan Everett, by his recollection, was one of the worst human beings that the earth had ever spat up—despite the goodness of his father's heart. Prosper didn't believe much in God or the Devil, but he did believe in good and evil and he knew that evil men walked among us—many with faces like angels. Roan had been just such a man. And the day that Keefe McCalister had put a bullet through Roan's throat only one man had wept.

Now, McCalister was dead, along with a good number of other folk that Roan had disliked or liked too much. And Prosper figured that being dead was not likely to stop a man such as Roan from his desires. There were some, Prosper knew, that believed only in the light of day and in what could be proven and seen. Scientific folks, he imagined, lived a comforted life knowing so little about what really was. The electric light, when it had come up and down the Valley, had shut out the shadows and put men's hearts to rest. But just because the dark was pushed back a bit didn't mean it was gone or that the things that lurked in the dark of night or in the dark of men's hearts were any less hungry.

It was plain to see the cause behind the slew of dead and disappeared that had come upon the valley. The fact that most folk didn't want to own what they already knew seemed a mystery to him. He had, in his sixty years, known dead folk to walk more than once. He had seen a crow speak with the voice of a girl and a river run red with blood. He had heard, in the high hills, the sultry sweet voice of the Wampus Cat and found prints left behind that matched no creature he could name. So when Alice Caldwell's mother came crying to his door in the dusk, saying her daughter had took missing, he knew what had to be done. Over the years, Vance had learned that truths, even the hardest ones to digest, had a certain taste to them. And despite the illogic of it, he could taste this truth clear down to the bone.

So, for the second time in that long week, he drove to the Everett place. Though this time the drive seemed longer, knowing what he might face at its end. Grief for certain lay ahead of him and perhaps something worse. As he walked the lonely path that led to the house, Prosper could see even through the growing gloom the old man waiting in his rocker on the covered porch. He climbed the stairs and when the old man did not move and he sat down at his right hand.

Old Man Everett sat staring out into the night for the longest time and then he began to rock again. "You know," he said simply to Prosper with a sigh. "I used to think that there was some right and wrong in this world. And that if a man did good, good would follow after."

"You ought to know better than that," Prosper said.

The old man nodded, "I do and yet I don't believe it. Don't want to. He was my son, and I knew him for what he was, but he was my son just the same."

"I never knew you to be a man that didn't stand by his principles," Prosper said, "None could say you didn't."

"You know what I am, I wager, and what I done for him." The old man said, "His death hit me hard. I come close to losing him as a boy more than once and it seemed some sort of mercy that he lived. With his mother gone, he was all I had. I wasn't there when he was shot. It could be that there was something that I could've done—even if it was only to make my peace with him."

"He lived his own life," Prosper said. "He was a man grown when he took that bullet. And though maybe you might've kept him from that bullet, there would've just been another on some other day."

"All our deaths are waiting for us one day or the other," the old man said. "Even mine."

"Still," Prosper said, "you did the best you could with that boy."

"It's a kindness for you to say it, but a boy follows after his father. He had, you see, his mother's heart. She was a wild thing, but I knew from the first time I clapped eyes on her that she was all I wanted." He chuckled and for a minute sounded almost young to Prosper, but then the moon passed by and he saw just how old the fellow was—ancient—almost as if he was cut from the earth and stones himself. "I might was well have loved a wild cat or a bear," he continued. "She wasn't something to be kept. And when the boy came and she died I turned all that love in on him and maybe it was too much for him to bear. Maybe it was too much for anyone to bear—to be so much to any other."

Prosper looked at him. "I don't conjure it was your fault. Every man comes up in this world one way or another and some are good and others aren't. A man has to take responsibility for what he does in this life."

"Yes," the old man said, "No truer words were spoken this day or any other. And that's what I mean to do."

"I wouldn't ask it of you. For whatever's he's done or is, he is your son."

"I brung him into this world twice. It lays on me to take him out of it." The old man smiled then, and laid his hand over Prosper's own, "You're a young man yet, so you might not know. But all men are called up out of the dirt—some stay in it a good while longer than others—but, in the end, all of them return to it. Nothing's to be done about it and sometimes it's a comfort to return to what we are. Dirt. Good and clean."

They sat in the dark, the old man rocking for a very long time. And softly, Prosper heard the old man say, "I, of all people, should've known better."

Hours passed before they heard the shuffling, heavy gait of stony dirt against the gravel path. Roan was coming home as he did each night. Under the full moon, Prosper could see that there was something dark smeared about his face and hands. He reeked of sorrow and sin and the old man rose to meet him. He walked down the path alone to meet his son and greeted him with a kiss. And softly, almost lip to lip, he whispered a word turned back on itself, almost too low for Prosper to hear—almost.

The change, from life to death, is not a quick one even if it lasts only lasts only a few seconds. And for the rest of his very long life Prosper would remember the old man on his knees in the dirt holding on to the rapidly dissolving form of his son. He would see, each night in his dreams, the slow silting of the clay and the rising piles of dust around the broken form of the old man until he was left holding only gleaming white bones tattered with linen. And even in his sleep, Prosper would weep.

Chapter 17:
Bluebeard's Wife

This is one of the stories that haunted my childhood. My Grandfather was a master storyteller and one of his favorites was Bluebeard's wife. I used to wait breathless, hoping that she wouldn't turn the key, hoping that somehow the reward for curiosity wasn't something sinister. Folks say curiosity kills the cat. But maybe sometimes the cat isn't the curious one.

Maggie James was a handsome woman with money to spare. She lived in a house, large and well-kept, by the shore. She was young yet to have been widowed at twenty-nine and younger still to have lost three husbands. But, it was true nonetheless. Folks said she was unlucky in love. And, though fortunate in all else, it did seem that Maggie and a husband were not meant to be. Her first husband was a captain almost twice her years. When he did abed, some felt sorry for the young woman, but few were surprised. Captain James had left young Maggie with a fine house, but no children. A pity. And, when she married in a year, it was only to be expected. She was young and a widow, and women have needs.

Maggie's second husband was the first mate on the schooner Pearl. He left twice a year on long voyages to the Islands and back again, and always brought Maggie a fine gift or two from his travels. But one day he didn't return. Folks reckoned he'd met foul play in a far harbor when he and his purse parted ways. Though his body was never recovered, such is the fate of men that go to sea. Maggie waited a full two years before she wed again, so there were none to question it. Many thought her brave – a woman alone in that house by the sea.

Maggie's third husband, by all accounts, was a scoundrel. A year or two her younger, Malcombe Davis had little to offer but his pretty face and his foul temper. Though he was a sailor, he took to drink and left the sea after he met Maggie. He took to spending his days lording it up in her fine house. When he left her for a barmaid at the Jolly Jim after only six months, most folks said it was good riddance. And, when he didn't return after a year or more, some said he was no doubt dead in a ditch and the world better for it. Maggie was alone again in her fine house. She walked the Widow's Walk in her house by the sea and watched the shore and for two years she did not marry again. Then, she met Elias.

Some say now his name was Percy or maybe even Robert, but I have it from the best sources that the young man's name was Elias. He was a sailor too, but it was a sailing town. A port. So that was only to be expected. But, young Elias was a first mate on a fine ship with a shining future and the manners of a gentleman. Many said he had a sad story behind him. A gentleman or even a nobleman who had fallen on hard times. Perhaps a family disgraced or fled for some indiscretion for which young men are always prone. But, for Maggie and Elias it was love at first sight. The red-haired widow and the raven-haired boy fell head over heels. And though Maggie was twenty-nine and a woman-grown, and Elias had just turned twenty, none doubted the match. Elias, for all his young years, was a quiet, stern fellow with eyes as grey as the sea. He seemed steady and devoted to Maggie. All the town said what a fine match it was, and how lovely that Maggie's bad luck had finally turned to good in matters of the heart.

But Elias, for all his good, dark looks, had a brooding heart. Sailors are often taken that way. For any man that loves the sea knows that she is a hard mistress – as often to wreck and drown a man as to carry him safely home. Elias took to following Maggie everywhere and even paid boys to follow her about town. If she spoke to another man, even a shopkeep, he fell into a black and furious mood. It took all of Maggie's doing to turn him to happier thoughts. But Maggie, used to inconstant men, took Elias' rages as a compliment. Still, the same folk that had praised the match and stood smiling at Maggie and Elias' wedding, murmured after a few months that the match would come to no good – that Maggie, poor soul, was as cursed as ever. Some said that it was Maggie herself that would go early to the grave this time instead of her groom and, most likely at his hand. But, Maggie, just smiled and shook her head. The more her young husband brooded and fumed the happier she seemed, as though fury was her bread and butter.

When Elias' ship was called to sea in the spring, Maggie stood on the Widow's Walk and watched him go all the time waving, though she knew the ship was too far out for any soul to see her. Long months passed before Elias returned, and many a letter he wrote to Maggie and she to him. Mostly, though, they kept them to themselves, hoping their beloved would read their missives at their reunion. A life at sea is a hard one. But, a life of waiting, if you ask most, is worse. For men go to sea and to war and ever to adventures, both fair and foul. But, it is a woman's place to wait and watch and wonder. And often, the news that comes to her is not hopeful. Still, after a year, Elias returned to Maggie and their reunion was merry. But, within a few weeks, Elias turned to his old suspicions. He told some friends of his that he believed Maggie was hiding something from him. But, they only laughed and said a woman was nothing but secrets, and he had no more to complain of that others and less than most. But Elias was not satisfied.

Elias knew that Maggie kept a tiny key on a silver chain about her neck. The key itself was not remarkable. But, the fact that she wore it ever, waking or sleeping, was a puzzle to him. He'd asked her once if not a hundred times about the mystery of the key. It was old and worn, too small for any doors that he knew of in the house. But, Maggie only laughed and told him it was the key to her heart. At first, the key seemed a light thing. It charmed him that Maggie had a secret. What could it be? He thought. Surely nothing more than a woman's whimsy. A key to some diary or box of sweet-nothings. But, as Elias' suspicions grew, so did his obsession with the key. After a time, he began to plague her day and night about it.

He followed her about hoping to see the secret of it. But, never, not once in all the months then years, did he see Maggie use the key. Once, while they idled in bed late in the morning and she was in a fair mood, he asked her prettily about it, as if it meant nothing to him. Maggie, smiling as he played with the dark curls of her hair, took the key from around her neck and held it to the light. "It is, as I have told you, the key to my heart," she said. "But, I've no use for it these days since my heart, as you know, my love, is in your keeping." Then she smiled sweetly and put the key back round her neck and lay back on the pillow with a laugh. "Would you strip me of all my secrets then, my love?" she asked, "For every woman has a heart of darkness and a soul that a man could never understand."

Elias took this for more of her evasion, though to her face he laughed and kissed her head. "I'd take you as you were, secrets or no," he said to her. But, in his heart, he resolved to know the secret of the key no matter the cost.

After that Elias doubled his watch and there was seldom a moment that he took his eyes from Maggie. If she ventured to the market on a sunny day with a basket on her arm, Maggie would find Elias not far behind her. If she woke in the night and tip-toed silently out to the Widow's Walk, she would turn only to find Elias standing still as a cat in the shadows. Once, when she thought she was alone on the shore, having taken a winding route, Maggie stood barefoot in the wash and sighed looking out to sea, only to hear her lover's breath behind her. "What is it you want?" she asked then, not angry, but only tired and a little sad. But, Elias said nothing and only stood staring at her in the dusk.

One night when the moon rode low in the sky, Elias watched as Maggie left the bed and closed the shutters. He lay, feigning sleep, until he heard her steps mouse-quiet in the hall. And, then he stood and followed behind her keeping always to the darkest shadows. Maggie crept to the library and moving one book and then another revealed a door he had never seen before. A door with a small and ancient frame and a hole just the right size for a small silver key. Her hand at her neck, Maggie turned and stood wild-eyed, her back to the door and the key clutched tight in her hand. And there in her shadow stood Elias.

"What is it?" he demanded. "Is this your secret, then? Where does it lead?" When she said nothing and stood staring and dull, he grabbed her by both shoulders and shook the woman. "I'll have it out of you yet," he wailed and threw her out of the way. The door held fast despite his kicks and beatings, so he turned to her, his eyes red with fury. "Give me that key," he said softly.

Then Maggie shook her head slowly. "No," she said, "but if you will, I will show you what I keep inside."

"What is it, then, a passage to your lover?" he cried.

Maggie looked him dead in the eyes and finally smiled her slow and secret smile. "As you say," she said, "it is the route I take to see my loves—every one of them." She pushed him then and put the key in the door and stepped back. "If you would lead, my love," she said. He stepped forward and turned the key. The door opened shyly it seemed to him, as if it had not been visited for some time. Behind him, he heard Maggie moan, and then the scrape of iron across the wooden floor.

The blow took him unexpected and he fell into the room catching himself only barely with a hand. It was dark and the smell was unpleasant. A waft of age and dust and something far worse. Behind him, he heard Maggie sigh, disappointedly as one would at a disobedient child. "You said you'd never leave me," she said. And, then, more quietly, "They all did."

As his eyes filled with the dark, he could see around him shapes unmoving and then Maggie's slender feet. She leaned down and caressed his cheek and then hit him once more hard on the brow with the poker than she held. "A pity," she said, running her hand around his stubbled chin, "I would've liked to have seen that beard. It's coming in so nice. Black and fine, almost blue in the light." She smiled again as his eyes grew dim. "I'll be back in an hour or so to see you again. You may see me then, or not. But, I will see you every day, my Love. And as you promised, you will never leave me alone." Maggie turned with a swirl of skirt and then he heard the door close and the rattling of the lock.

He lay alone, but not alone, in the dark and tried not to think of the dark pool growing around his head or the numb feeling in his hands. He turned his head slowly and saw not far from him what must've been Maggie's first husband, or perhaps her second. Maybe a lover. Who could tell now? Even in death, the boy looked young, yellow hair streaming mercifully across his ruined face. Maggie had caught him by surprise too, because even from here, he could see the glint of a dagger's hilt protruding from his boot. A sailor's boot.

Maggie would be back in an hour or so, so she said. And, by then, perhaps, he would be able to crawl across the room and take the dagger in hand. One way or another, they'd always be together. He smiled and the dust moved around him as he sighed and tried to rise on one hand. For what seemed like an eternity he crawled toward the boy, the boot and the dagger. At times he lay breathing heavy on the floor and then moved again. Always toward the boot. The room was shadowless. No windows to mar the perfect dark and only the light from under the door as a guide. A room full of lovers and enemies, and lovers who were enemies, kept close and safe and secret and forever. If only no one asked for the key. If only no one ever turned the lock. If only the door remained closed. He reached for the dagger and found it cold in his hand. The key turned in the door and in the dry, hallowed dark he smiled and waited for his love to meet him.

Chapter 18:
The Baba Yaga of Fox Chase

The South is full of witches, and most of them probably aren't what you'd expect. A good deal of them probably won't call themselves witches at all, although they might tell a fortune with coffee grounds, have a few tricks to bring on a rainstorm, or know the right herbs to mend a broken bone or a broken heart. Folk tales and fairy stories are around every corner and under every stone. So, you should probably be careful just whose flower beds you decide the trample.

"She's a witch," Tim said standing with one sneakered foot on his skateboard, the other on the street. He used his cupped hand to shield his eyes from the noonday glare as he peered sunward at the house's garden. "Naah," said Mike, "She don't look like any witch I ever saw." He popped a bubble of grape gum and smiled.

"You idiot," said Tim, "Whattayathink, she'd go around with warts and a pointy hat? Don't you ever watch TV? They look like everyone else now." Tim's mother watched *Charmed* on Netflix so he considered himself an expert on this point.

Mike squinted his eyes in consideration. "Naah, she's not even old as my Mom." Tim tipped the skateboard back down and tapped it once in exasperation. "You are a dope," he said, "She's a witch for sure. 'Course she's not old or warty. If you had magic, would you go 'round with warts and wrinkles?"

Mike studied the house. It did look sort of witchy. The trees were old and dark, and ivy coated one side of the stone cottage. He tilted his head. The roof looked lop-sided too—like the house was somehow grinning at him. It seemed friendly, like a big cat. He shook his head, "Doesn't she write that plant column for the newspaper?"

Tim rolled his eyes. "So she can't write stuff and be a witch, huh? Doesn't your Mom do accounting, and still fix homeless lunches for the church? Maybe she's a witch plus other stuff."

"I suppose," Mike agreed, "She gave me a caramel apple last Halloween." Tim stared his eyes gone small and dark. "It was good with nuts on top," Mike continued.

"I don't see what that has to do with anything," said Tim tapping the skateboard again.

"I thought they poisoned apples—like in Snow White," Mike observed.

Tim sighed, "That's just cartoons. Besides, the Wicked Witch didn't go 'round poisoning everyone, right? Just Snow White."

Mike nodded, "She sure was dumb to take that apple after the comb and all that other stuff."

"You ate your apple," Tim said smirking.

"It had nuts on it," Mike said. They both stood and examined the house further. Inside, they could see a dark shape moving in front of the gauzy, wine-colored curtains. "So what if she is a witch?" said Mike. "I don't reckon we could do anything about it."

"Doesn't seem right," said Tim, "Letting witches go 'round doing stuff and all."

"What stuff?" asked Mike.

"Just stuff," said Tim. "I guess she'd be up to all sorts of stuff. Curdling milk and causing skateboards to chip for no reason. Stuff. Just stuff for fun."

Mike looked at him. "Why?" he asked.

Tim sighed again, "Because she could. Wouldn't you, if you could? I'd do all sorts of stuff. Like fly away the school and turn all the orange juice to Pepsi. Stuff like that." Mike nodded. Tim's hatred of his mandatory glass of orange juice each morning was legendary.

"Must be nice," Mike said. He kicked the skateboard and looked back at Tim. "Come on," he said, "*Super Power Patrollers* is on, I think." Mike nodded and the two boys headed down the street. The curtain in the house's front window opened a slit. Anyone watching would have seen a tiny furred paw and then a pink nose.

Behind the cat, the pale-haired woman in running shorts stretched on the couch. She waved her hand and the TV flashed from *Oprah* to another talk show. "Well," she said, "did you hear anything useful?" The cat shook his head and jumped down off the armchair. He stretched twice and sauntered into the kitchen. "Get me something while you're in there, will you?" the woman called after the cat.

"Yes, Baba," the cat murmured petulantly from the kitchen.

Baba Yaga kicked off her house slippers and waved on her Toshiba laptop. It started with a low growl. "Write something for that newspaper," she said, "And, don't sap it up so much this time." The laptop began its low clicking and Baba reached for a bag of chips. There was nothing on TV – as usual. She tapped her foot in agitation on the floor, and underneath her the house shifted its long legs. She smiled. Some things never change. She patted the floor affectionately and the house settled back on its foundation.

In her kitchen she could hear her oven popping. It looked like a Kenmore range, but in its day it had seen more exotic fare than the pot pie she planned to cook for her dinner. Baba walked to the kitchen and saw the cat opening the cupboard. She looked over the sink and down into her garden. "Damn that mole," she said, "I'll get him tonight." She could see from here that her chrysanthemums were lop-sided from his tunneling. She grabbed a pot pie from the freezer and put it in the oven. The oven made a happy little sniff like a playful dog. Baba saw that the cat was now sitting on the ledge drinking cream straight from the container. Her own drink was nowhere to be seen. The cat eyed her insolently as he drank. She reached in the refrigerator and pulled out a Diet Pepsi, letting the door slam. The cat pretended not to hear.

Baba Yaga walked back to the living room and plopped back down on the couch. On TV some actress was extolling the virtues of Wicca and Kabbalah for inner peace. Baba snorted and drank her Pepsi. "Maybe I should get one of those pentacles. What do you think, cat?" She called back toward the kitchen. The cat, who never had many manners, didn't bother to answer. Baba flipped the channel again. She could hear the low murmur of the house as it settled for a nap. Baba yawned. Maybe she could do for a nap, too. The potpie would be ready when she woke up. She smiled. These days, dreams were more interesting than life. You couldn't even take your house for a walk without causing a ruckus.

Baba curled up, tucking her knees near her chest, and in no time she was dreaming. Down the street, Mike and Tim flipped on *Super Power Patrollers* and ate cookie dough straight from the roll. The mole knocked over a stand of lavender and ate three tulip bulbs. At six o'clock the street lights came on and the little timer on Baba's oven chimed. Baba stretched and got up. Her pot pie was ready.

"What should we do tonight, cat?" Baba asked, taking her dinner from the oven.

"Don't care," said the cat. His nose was covered in cream.

"Wipe your face," said Baba.

"You're one for manners all of a sudden," said the cat jumping down and not wiping his face.

"Do something useful for once and kill that mole," said Baba. The cat, without reply, popped through the cat door. From the window, Baba could see him leaving the yard and sauntering down the street. Baba took a bite of the pot pie. The center was cold. She glared at the oven. "Center's cold, again!" she said. The oven made a sad little whimper and clicked back on. She shoved the pot pie back in and slammed the oven door.

Sulkily, Baba went back to the couch and picked up the newspaper. Flipping to the real estate section she eyed the ads for condominiums. Everyone said they were the height of convenience and maybe she could find one that didn't allow pets. Under her feet she could feel the house sigh in its sleep. She patted the floor again. She could put up with the Cat for a bit yet, she thought. "I'll feel better once I have my dinner," she said aloud.

Baba curled her legs underneath her and flipped on the TV once again. "Ahh, the news, just like old times," she said. At least someone out there was still creating mayhem. "Retirement's not as appetizing as they say," she murmured. The oven dinged again and she smiled, "Good," she said, "it's finally done".

Chapter 19:
Things At The Bottom Of The Well

There are always things at the bottom of an old well. Things in the dark. You can't quite see them and you don't quite want to.

Roses and coins
Wishes and lockets
These things fell down the well.
Stones loosened by time
Change from his pocket
All at the bottom of the well.
Darkness and light
Shadow and spite
Trace patterns on the walls of the well.
Pity and hope
Love and remorse
All in tatters at the bottom of the well.
Broken and bent
Hope nearly spent
Draped in sorrow in the dark, in the well.
Fingernails break
There's no choice left to make
Only wait in the black, sit and wait.
In the deep and the dank
Dreams have risen and sank
To the bottom of this abandoned ole well.

Chapter 20:
End Of The Road

There are things that live in shadows and only come when they're called. The trouble is you don't always know when you've called them.

"A witch lives at the end of the road," Erica said. "It's true. No one ever sees her, but sometimes she comes out, when no one looking."

"If she only comes out when no one's looking," Robin said, "then how do you know she comes out at all?"

"Well, because sometimes people just disappear. They go missing and no one finds anything except maybe gristle and old bones. Not enough to even know it was a person."

"Then, how do they?" I asked., "Know it was, I mean."

"They just do," Erica said. "Ask anyone. Ask my brother or anyone. Everyone knows."

It didn't sound likely. I mean, if there was a witch that lived down the road that was snatching up people and turning them into stew bones, you'd think everyone would know and someone would do something about it. But, then again, there were more than a few things that there should be a remedy for that were just overlooked or ignored flat out. So, for all I knew, maybe there were witches down just about every road making off with folks, merry as you please, with no one to do a thing about it.

Or maybe Erica was lying. She did that a lot. But sometimes she told the truth just to keep you on edge. So, you never knew when she was making something up outright, stretching the facts a bit, or telling it true and plain. Sometimes the truth is hard to recognize, especially when you're a girl of ten fed on stories of Wampus cats and hoop-snakes, a girl who

103

knew that an owl hooting by day brought bad luck, or rain, or a combination of the two. Life, legend, and lies have a way of bleeding together like a pot of gumbo when you're a kid. You can't tell okra from crawfish when a deep roux is stirred over them all.

Robin and I were dubious. Here was Erica squinting her eyes at the sun and twisting her foot in the dirt, sure signs of deceit. But Dana and Susan, three years younger than the youngest of us, were round-eyed with interest and far down the road to belief. Erica, with the heart of a true storyteller or a door-to-door salesman, directed her tale to the more receptive audience. "Once," she said dropping her voice to a near whisper so we all had to lean forward a bit, "She followed me all the way home. It was late and I was riding my bike, but the chain got stuck, so I had to push it home. I felt her watching me when I went past her house, so I pushed the bike past as fast as I could. That's when I felt it."

"Felt what?" Susan asked, twisting her braid round and round.

"I could feel her eyes on me," Erica said, "Like two ice cubes on the back of my neck. And then I could hear her following. I couldn't see her, but I could hear the bones."

This being a new development in the story, Robin and I were intrigued. "So, she's, like what?" Robin asked, "A skeleton or something?"

"No," Erica said, summoning all the scorn a ten-year-old could muster, "she wears them. She wears all the bones of the people she eats."

"I thought she left them in the woods," I said. "You know, so people could find them. That's what you said."

"No, I didn't," Erica said with a smirk, "I said folks find bones and gristle, but that's just from the ones she doesn't eat. The best ones she keeps and then she stews them up and then she wears their bones."

"Like a dress?" Robin asked. "That doesn't seem very comfortable. You can get a dress down at Penney's for ten dollars. I don't see why she'd wear bones."

"I didn't SAY it was a dress," Erica replied. "I just said she wears them—like a necklace or in her hair. No one really knows 'cause no one sees her, but they hear her. They hear the bones."

It sounded like a pack of nonsense to me and I could see by the way Robin was raising an eyebrow and tapping her foot she thought it was hokum as well. But then we heard it—a rattle like a branch against a window or a mortar against a glass bowl. It was a scrape and a rattle together and something else too—a sly little slithering sound like a snake moving across dry leaves. I felt a coldness like a finger go up my spine, and Susan and Dana grabbed each other's hand.

We looked right and left, but there was nothing—just a shaded road at the end of the day with an overhang of old elm and birch trees, and pavement gone gray in patches. Erica shrugged toward the end of the road to the old house. From where we stood, it was nothing but clapboards gone to termites and a rickety old porch that probably couldn't bear a grown man's weight. The yard was a mess of weeds and brambles with a twisted crab apple tree heavy with black spotted fruit and covered in kudzu and ivy. There was a rope swing that had half given way years ago so that the seat hung low in the dirt on one frayed rope. When the wind kicked up it gave a half-hearted swing and you could hear something metal moving in the distance. It had a rusted, creaking sound you could almost imagine was whispering your name.

"Just an old house," Robin said. "Nothing's there."

"You heard it!" Erica said in a whispering hiss, "I know you heard it."

"Heard what?" I asked. "Just something rusted. Probably an old gate or a broken hinge."

"It was bones," she said. And just then we did hear it. We heard that low rattle and hiss that we'd heard earlier coming from the woods to the right of the house, not close, but closer than it was before.

Dana let out a little sniffle. And Robin snorted.

"She knows," Erica said. "She heard us talking and now she knows!" And without another word she turned heel and started running flat out toward home.

We stood staring at her for a minute. She could run fast when she wanted to, there was no doubt about that. Dana and Susan suddenly took off after her. I looked at Robin and she looked at me, and then we glanced behind us. Woods, an old house, and the wind. Then there was that noise. Rattle, rattle, hiss. Rattle, rattle, hiss. RATTLE, RATTLE, HISS. And we ran.

We ran as fast as our size ten tennis shoes could carry us. We ran until our breath was rattling in our chests in little starts and stops. We ran until we caught up with Susan and Dana and we could see Erica on the porch of her house. She grabbed the screen door and let it fly back with a snap. It hit the wall hard and I caught it on the rebound.

We all piled inside and latched the screen and then closed the heavy door behind us. I locked it three times, two deadbolts and the lock turn on the door knob. Peering through the chintz curtains on the door window, pressed together as tight as sardines in a tin, we could see how dark it had gotten all of the sudden. It does that in late October, when the days are growing long and the leaves start to turn. A day can turn to dusk in the time it takes you to walk to the mailbox. And although we'd run in the low light of the afternoon, it was full dusk now and you could see the shadow of a moon. The shadows at the end of the drive were heavy and full and you could see them move every time the wind started up.

"She's right there," Erica said, pointing to a patch of dark to the left of the drive where the mailbox might have been. "See her? Down low, on her hands and knees like a cat."

We peered in the dark. We didn't dare turn on the porch lights and in the late shadows you could almost see it, her. Something low to the ground like a dog or a calf. Something more made of shadow than flesh. Something watching. And you could feel it. You could feel a cold dread like a fingernail scraping down your cheek. Like tears of ice.

"She knows we're here alone," Erica said. "She knows and she'll turn us into bones."

"Get in the bathroom," I said. "We can just hide. She doesn't know we're here and if she did then she can't get in."

But I didn't know if I believed that. What if she was a witch or worse? What if she was some kind of a haint that could slither through door and frame? What if she was the kind of thing that drinks in shadows and could pull herself up through a drain or flatten herself like a mouse and creep under the door? I grabbed my little sister's hand which was sweaty with that icy undertone that fear can give you and pushed her and Dana into the bathroom. Erica and Robin came in last and Robin turned the lock. Dana and Susan had already crawled in the bathtub and pulled down the towels as a sort of cover. I started opening cabinets while Erica hissed "Be quiet!" and "She'll hear us!"

There was nothing. Just a flyswatter and a plunger. I handed the plunger to Robin, and then Erica, Robin and I knelt on the cold linoleum with our ears pressed to the door. Our breathing was as loud as the hum of the bathroom's fluorescent lights. I could feel Robin's curly hair against my cheek and Erica's breath each time she whispered, "Can you hear it?" And we could. We could hear it. We heard the front door rattle and shake. We heard the locks give way with a pop, pop, pop and then we heard footsteps light and sly. Finally, we heard the bones.

God help me, we heard them. We heard the rattle and hiss of old bones sliding together and a dry little noise like dry leaves crumbling that I took to be her breath. And then we heard and saw the door knob twist. It twisted one then twice then another time. And we heard scratches on the door like a cat that wanted to be let in. Tentative at first and then insistent. We heard the scratches and we felt them, even though we had our back to the door and our feet braced against the counter. Dana and Susan lay under the towels whimpering and Robin's hand on the plunger was white as snow. We heard the knob twist and twist and twist and then the scratches again and again until I thought we would all start screaming. Erica started to laugh. Not a nice laugh, but a high strange one. She had her eyes closed and her feet propped against the cabinet. Three little sets of shoes all dusty with different color shoestrings.

I can remember our shoes to this day. I remember how my feet where a size bigger than the rest and Robin's shoe strings were purple with sparkles. I remember the way the handle of the flyswatter bit into my hand and the way the door felt, cold and fiery, at the same time. I remember how the scratches sounded and how I could almost feel them through the wood. Like they were scratching our flesh and not just the door; and I remember how suddenly they stopped. They just stopped. And it was like we could suddenly breathe. I was aware of Dana's hiccupping tears and Robin's sigh beside me. We slowly turned and put our hands on the door, then our ears, and we heard nothing. Nothing. We could hear the heater in the house click on the way it does with a low murmur, and somewhere you could hear a clock ticking. But there was nothing else.

I don't know how long we sat there. It seemed like hours, but maybe it was only minutes. We pushed back away from the door and watched it like a cat stares down a snake, and finally I stood, unlocked the door, and with a shaking hand opened it. Years later, someone asked me what was the bravest thing I'd ever done in my life and I replied, "I opened a door." I think they thought I meant it as a metaphor. I didn't. I have never, in my life, been as afraid as I was the day I opened that door. I remember the twists in the grain of the wood and how the iron of the old knob felt in my hand. I remember how the door hung a little when I opened it and how my sneaker slipped on the floor when I gave it a tug and I remember what I saw. Nothing. An empty hallway with an ordinary rug.

When our parents came to pick us up that night, Susan and Dana were in a state and Robin and I got an earful for playing along with Erica. But it wasn't a trick. I don't think it was even a trick or a story to Erica after a while. She believed, too. We all believed.

And she's still there, waiting, the witch and her bones in her house at the end of the road. She's still waiting in the dark and the shadows for a little girl or a little boy to call her to hear her bones and their rattle, to feel the scratch of her bony fingers through the wood, to be carried off into the shadows never to return.

Chapter 21:
Wolf Run

I always found fairy tales disturbing as a child. Not because I was afraid of them being true. I was certain they were true and also fairly sure they fairies wouldn't like the things being said.

Ghost stories aren't about happy endings. There are no happy endings once a story has ended. And, let's face it, for the primary character in the ghost story, the ghost him or herself, the story is over. Whether they're trying to redress a wrong, find their way home, or just stop by for a visit, a spirit's story is in the past tense. But fairy tales, on the other hand, are all about the present. They're happening right now. All around us. With endings that are both happy and sad and everything in between.

Fairy tales are more than the stuff of legend, they are the backbone of the everyday. Every child believes in them. Fairies are what you see in the corner of your eye. They're the ones that threw your doll down the well, stole the cat's milk, and blew the fuse box right before your favorite show was about to air. Fairies are all around us and they aren't nice. They're the ones that hide in the tall grass. They pull at you in deep water. They bar the way home.

There are things in the dark and they're waiting. They don't have names and if they ever did, they forgot them a very long time ago. Maybe they've lived forever in the shadows, hungry and waiting, or maybe they're brand new. It doesn't matter because they are. They are and they're waiting. You can feel them like little pricks of ice on your skin. You feel them when you walk a lightless country road. You feel them when you have to check the root cellar without even a candle to guide your way. They're in the corner where the light doesn't shine and in the crack where the closet door opens. You know what they want better than they do. They want everything. They want to gobble you up and leave no bones. And sometimes they do. It doesn't matter what your parents tell you. It doesn't matter what you tell yourself. They're still there and sometimes you don't make it home.

When I was a little girl my grandmother had a Time-Life book. It had all sorts of stories. Toads encased in coal and stone for a hundred years that croaked when the stone was cracked. Blue children found speaking languages that no one knew or remembered. Folks that burst into flames leaving behind unsinged cups of coffee and fluffy slippers. And those that just up and disappeared. Those were the worst. Those were the stories that haunted me because you heard them before. You heard them all the time. Some hunter went out in the fields and never came back. Or a dog that took off running across a field and disappeared right before his master's eyes. Doll dresses that went under the edge of the chifferobe and weren't there when you reached in to get them. Empty spots. They didn't bear thinking about. If a dog or a doll or a man could fall into one, so could you.

But where did they fall? Where did they go? Sometimes they came back, in stories, maybe in real life too, dazed and wild-eyed—years gone by and they not changed a bit, or a day gone by and they seemingly aged years. Gone to places that don't have names or time. Places like dreams and nightmares or something a bit like both. Gone into fairytales. And usually not coming back.

There's a road called Wolf Run not far from my parent's house. No one has seen a wolf in Tennessee in a hundred years—maybe more. But one day, more than forty years ago, a wolf appeared on the hill above the stone wall that marks the graveyard. He seemed as surprised as anyone. He appeared for a week running, just standing on the hill. No one saw him leave or show up. Appeared was the only word for it. He seemed dazed, dazzled. He didn't run or snarl. He just was. Maybe he was rabid or lost. Folks never knew. Or maybe he stepped out of a world full of wolves into one that had none.

That can happen. One minute you're standing in your own backyard or walking across a field and the next you find yourself in a place that isn't the same. Who hasn't been in the woods, woods they knew each and every tree and then looked up and nothing was familiar? In times like those all you can do is keep walking and hoping, with your dog huddled against your legs and a look in her eyes that says, "I hope you know the way home, because I surely do not."

There are things that lie in darkness, watching and waiting. They never die because they've never rightly been alive. They have teeth of stone and eyes like knives. They're hungry. They're always hungry. Because they can never be filled. Dogs and children know this truth. They know to be afraid of the dark because there's plenty to fear. But somewhere along the way adults forget—or convince themselves they have. They convince themselves to ignore that whispering in the back of their mind, the cold on the nape of their neck, that old dark part of their brain that says "Go back, go back!" They tell themselves there's no witch at the end of the road, no boogie man under the bed, but what if they're wrong?

They may even know it, but perhaps it is easier to simply get up, go to work and live your life believing that daylight is the truth and darkness is the lie—when you know in you truest heart that it's always darkness. We don't know much, and what we do know is a child's make-believe. There are old things. Things in the dark. They wait and watch and mostly they're content. But every now and again they come out to play, and they don't play nice. If you see a dog turn tail and run at a shadow or a cat hiss at a dark corner, best to avoid it. Best to find iron and silver and water. Best to shine a light. Because small things know when the faeries are hungry. Small things have never lost that wary edge. They know when a shadow is a pool of darkness and when it's the cloak for something hungry. They know when to back and edge. They know when to run.

It's something to remember the next time you're walking down a dark flight of stairs, pulling the hallway door closed, or decide to take a shortcut in the dark. You never know what's waiting for you around the corner. It's something to think on when you feel those fine hairs at the back of your neck stand and the palms of your hand go cold. There are things waiting and they don't mind it one bit, because they can wait forever. They can wait for the moment you aren't paying attention. They're the shadows that flit in the corner of your eye, that door that you swear just opened a bit, and the breeze on your cheek when the air is still. They're waiting now and forever. Can you hear them almost silent only, a breath or a sigh? Can you feel them watching you like little knives on the back of your neck? Can you feel their icy fingers reaching out just to fill a moment of warmth before they drag you into their cold, cold world? You know you can.

It's bad luck to speak ill of the dead and worse luck to speak ill of faeries. Names are things of power. Words have a way of calling things to you—for better or worse. To speak of a thing, to think of a thing is to bring it full into the light. Stories are like that. They contain a spell, and when you read them, they bring it to life. But you have to keep reading even when you're too frightened to turn the pages, even when your fingers are clammy and you can't feel the edges of the page. You have to read right to the end. That's how they catch you, you know. They wait for you to turn the corner, open the door, read the next page and then you're caught. You might not even realize it and before you know it an hour is gone or two or three. Little sips of time drawn right out of you.

But you'll keep reading, won't you? Because it's lonely here in the dark.

113

Chapter 22:
Stained

A wound never really heals even when the mark of it is gone. It stays with you under the skin and in your mind. Its passage creates something new for better or for worse. And even if you move on, even if you forget, some part of it stays behind as a reminder.

The house was old, but solid with a wide front porch and square columns. It had red brick walls with a stone foundation and curls of ivy that had eaten into the brick. There were windows, so many windows, of old dark glass that cast heavy shadows on the wooden floors of the front rooms. Trees hung low over the drive and a garden, overrun, but so beautiful, filling one side of the backyard. You could find hollyhocks and pumpkin, okra and onions, roses and garlic, and even real cotton that hung in little desultory tuffs. Persimmon and cherry trees cast their small, sour fruit on ground near the edge of the garden, and you could find the peach trees by the buzz of the bees. Rabbits chewed the lily and daffodil bulbs and left them strewn on the back porch in spring and early autumn, and wasps made their nests in the eaves around the porch.

But it was cold. Even in the high summer, the house was cold, and no wonder, Papa told her. In its heyday, all five fireplaces would've been burning in the winter, and folks would've taken bed warmers and more than a few quilts with them to bed. As it was, the house was bearable, but just, in the summer, and terrible in the winter. It would've been easier to close off the top floor and sleep in the main rooms on the bottom floor. After all, there were only the six of them, and a floor of rooms was more than they could've have hoped for a year, or even five years ago. Nell remembered sleeping in tenant cabins with spaces in the slat boards big enough to fit a cat through, and roofs that shuddered with each storm and wept with each rain. This house was solid and big and, once Momma had her way with lye and scrub brush, clean. But there were some stains that just wouldn't come up no matter how hard you scrubbed.

Deep, dark patterns overlaid the wood on the bottom two floors and the room at the top of the stairs. Smudges appeared on the stairs that no amount of wood polish or ash could remove. The house had old wounds, wounds that had never healed, wounds that would never heal. Momma found a big rag rug and covered the front parlor floor and over a summer Nell and her sister, Sarah, wove a grass rug for the back room. That was good, much better, but it didn't change the fact the stains were there. Papa tried painting over them, even though it wasn't allowed in the tenant's lease, but it was still no good. You couldn't quite see the stains, but they were still there, seeping through like little patches of mud. Nell wasn't going to sleep on them and neither was Sarah, and even if her brothers said they didn't mind, she'd find them creeping up the stairs and curling up in the cold with Sarah and Nell. Better to be cold than to be there with all that sadness. It was like the house was weeping.

And it wasn't just the stains. There were whispers. Sometimes you didn't even notice it, but every now and then if you walked into a room too quickly you would hear the talking stop. But they weren't too bad once you got used to them. They even seemed polite the way they'd stop when you came around the corner, like a child caught out doing something naughty. It was the crying that Nell couldn't stand. It was a soft, quiet crying like a child's and it went on and on. It broke Nell's heart every time she heard it. She just wanted to run and wrap her arms around the whole house and tell it that it would be okay, that the war was over and had been over for near a hundred years, that all the folks that suffered were gone on to some other place. At least that's what she hoped. But sometimes she'd see them, a soldier standing in a corner, a woman in a white dress, fuzzy forms in the garden reaching for peaches. She hoped there had been peaches then and persimmons and sweet corn on the stalks. She hopes that they'd lit fires on dark nights and ate corn hot in its shucks and laughed as much as they ever cried. She tried to tell herself they had, but she didn't believe it. She never believed it because at night the house would cry.

One day when Nell was in the springhouse, she looked up and saw a girl's face in the high window of the old house. She thought she was smiling and when Nell waved, she waved back. Nell wondered about the girl for a long time. She wondered if she were a ghost, or if somehow she was looking out from her own time and wondering about the strange girl coming out of the springhouse in a worn blue dress with boots two sizes too big. Nell shoved rags in the toes, but they were still too big, but that was okay. Too big boots were better than no boots at all, which Nell knew full well.

Nell bet that the girls that lived in this house when it was built never had to worry about putting rags in the toes of their boots or patching the elbows of their coats each winter. She reckoned they had maids to put all their dresses right and when something was too small or wore out, they just moved on to something better. Even so, she knew in her heart, that she wouldn't change places with them for all the dresses and shoes and dolls in the world. She only had one raggedy ole doll named Ann, and Sarah had another she called Miss Bess. Both of them had button eyes and their yarn hair had seen better days. Once she had seen a porcelain doll in store window in a stiff white dress that stuck out in every direction. Nell reckoned it was the sort of dolls that the little girls in this house might've had. They'd surely worn dresses as fine as any dolls, sat in polished mahogany chairs and eaten with real silver spoons. Maybe they took carriage rides down the long drive and played with kittens on the wide back porch, and made corn wreaths in the garden.

But they also would've seen more than a thousand soldiers laid to rest in their own yard under the dark trees, fields burned, and hedges hacked through, with the air turned thick with blood and ash and sorrow. When Nell thought about it too much, she'd go into the garden and cry. Sometimes she cried for a long time and one time she felt someone take her hand. She thought it was Sarah sitting beside her until she finished wiped her eyes with her fist and saw it was no one at all. But she wasn't scared. She felt thankful and hoped that maybe somewhere back in time that little girl from the window was sitting under a tree and if she was crying that maybe she could feel her hand.

Nell's brothers were less keen on the house than the girls. They complained about all the firewood they had to cut in winter and that the fields were filled with stones. It didn't matter how many you picked out each spring, a new crop would surface by the autumn. The ground spat stones, Nell's father said, and so it did. Maybe that's why the place was called Carnton. Mama told Nell that it meant place of stones. But her brother, Billy, five years old and cruel by nature, whispered, that it really meant place of gravestones. Nell was sure he was right, but she didn't tell Sarah, even if she already knew that as truly as did Nell. This was a place of graves, a place where the dead walked, a place where spirits spoke. But it was still better than a shanty house or no house at all.

Papa said the fields were fine and that you could grow most anything you put a mind to if you put enough blood and sweat into it. And Mama said the spring was one of the clearest she'd ever seen, and the well had good clear water even when rains were low. Nell and Sarah loved the garden and the trees. They loved the wide porch with wisteria hanging in low clumps that smelled like every good thing you could imagine in the summer, and the smooth floor of the springhouse where you could stretch out if you got too hot running and take a long nap. And they loved the little girl in the window even if they didn't know her name and she'd never know theirs. They hoped that she loved them, too. It was a good house even if there were bad memories left in the stone and wood, because there were good memories there, too.

Chapter 23:
Wampus

There are a thousand different tales about witches, but one thing lies at the heart of them all. A witch is never satisfied. Want is at the center of all witchcraft. A witch is the kind of person who doesn't take no for an answer even when it's given by fate and nature and all the forces that be. A witch looks destiny in the eye and spits.

Of course, there's a drawback to spinning the wheel of fate again and again. And every witch knows that his or her number may come up at any minute. You can meddle with the rhyme and scheme of things, sure enough, if you have the will to do it. But that doesn't mean that you won't be meddled with in return. Nature has a way of righting itself. And like a rubber band stretched too tight, sometimes it's only a question of when and whether it will rebound or just snap clean in two.

Once there was an old woman who thought she knew better than everyone else. This was, most likely, because she did. She was clever and could talk riddles around most folks, but that wasn't enough. She liked to get the upper hand even when she was wrong. And on the rare occasion that she couldn't twist a situation to her liking with her sweet words, she'd brood on it. Sometimes, after a day or two of sulking, she'd forget the whole thing. Other times, she'd slip out in the night like a shadow to the woods where she'd drop her skin into a little hole she'd dug just to keep it, and then she'd twist herself into a new shape.

Sometimes she was an owl, sometimes a cat, and sometimes a fox. She liked to be small and quiet and quick. Once she was in her new shape, she'd run through the woods to the house of the person that had vexed her and she'd wait. If she could, she'd find some way in the house or the barn to work some mischief. But, if they were sensible folk and hung iron above their door or kept salt at their window sill, then she'd sit twitching her tail and just listen at their window. You'd be surprised what folk will say when they think they're alone.

She used the information you found out listening at keyholes and doors for her own advantage. And sometimes there was a great deal of advantage to be had. She knew when people were in need of a loan or doing well, she knew when a child was on the way or a family was planning to sell their land, and she knew things that no one wanted her or anyone to know. She knew secrets that folks were desperate to keep silent. Sometimes she kept these secrets, and sometimes she let them slip out silent and sure as cats. But whatever she did, it was to her advantage.

Folks in town thought she was blessed. She never seemed to have any ill luck, her well never went dry or muddy, her cows gave the most milk in the county, and she never was sick a day in her life. Folks thought her uncanny, but there were plenty of men and women about who could predict a rain or bring one, save a sick child or calf, and tell your fortune from coffee grounds cast on the ground. But it was more than just that. There was an oddness about her that went beyond the uncanny. She stood apart as if she knew she was better than everyone else. There was just a feeling that she was laughing at everyone, and often she was.

There was a certain drover who lived on the edge of town that kept donkeys. He had twelve fine beasts that he would lend out for a price or in trade. Each one was named for an apostle, save the last one who was named Jasper after the drover himself to avoid ill fate. Jasper, the man not the donkey, was tall and broad-bellied with a voice to match. He liked a good smoke and a good drink and a good laugh best of all. He liked dogs and donkeys and had a keen understanding of the animal mind. Folks would, on occasion, come to him with questions about horses and cows and other critters. After all, if a man can get good service from a passel of donkeys, a troublesome horse would be no bother at all.

Donkeys have hearts of iron and hooves to match. There's no reasoning with a donkey. He only understands force of will and few in the world could match their willpower against donkey with a set mind. But Jasper could out-donkey any donkey going. He had a stare that would set coon dogs howling and some folks said would set the Devil himself running. He had a way of looking at and through things that even a donkey could respect.

Jasper was, on the whole, a good natured fellow who was content to laugh his way through life. It was his big, careless laugh that first brought him to the Witch's attention and it immediately set her teeth on edge. Here was a fellow, she knew, that was not to be hood-winked.

In a small town, the Witch and Jasper would've met much earlier, but country folks are a solitary lot. They met at need and at church and that was the long and short of it. For that reason, the two had no reason to cross paths for many years although each had, no doubt, heard of the other. Maybe nature herself had kept them apart like the ends of a magnet knowing that no good could come from a meeting. But, as it were, on a Sunday as the Witch was holding court outside on the church steps and dazzling everyone with her knowledge of herbs and sundries, Jasper's lead donkey, Peter, decided to kick down the barn door and take a stroll down the road. This might've been fine on a Wednesday or Thursday or even a Saturday afternoon when no one was about. But Peter, like any right-minded donkey, was drawn to a commotion and before long he ended up at the church. He immediately took a shine to the Witch's horse and before the entire congregation began to romance her. Jasper arrived just in time to see the Witch beating his prize donkey, to no great effect, with her willow cane and shouting out some choice words no lady should know, let alone utter in front of a church.

The loss of her composure, along with her horse's virtue, was too much the Witch to bear. She cast a withering look at Jasper, an evil eye of such venom that any creature would've begged her forgiveness, but Jasper just laughed. He gave his donkey a wallop on the flanks and told the Witch she could expect a fine mule, which he'd be glad to purchase as it would likely put even Peter to shame. The Witch was not amused. She narrowed her eyes until only the slightest glint could be seen and turned on heels so sharply that the boots gouged out little crescents in the packed clay. From that day on, she and Jasper were at war, whether he knew it or not.

That very night the Witch ran to the woods, shimmied out of skin, and set off for Jasper's farm. But donkeys are not easily shaken. No amount of shapeshifting or hokum had any effect on the donkeys. The Witch could've sworn that Peter smirked at her as she leaned panting against the fence after her fifth shift. And, since Jasper kept only donkeys and mules, there was no other mischief to be made on his farm—no milk to sour, no crops to wilt, and no wells to dry. The donkeys drank from the stream, ate from the field, and Jasper bought his hay from folks in town, including some from the Witch's own fields. It was a troublesome situation all around.

Next, the Witch tried turning herself into a mouse and listening at Jasper's keyholes and window. She listened for three days running and then took the risk of creeping inside seeing as there was no horseshoe above his door or witch's glass hung to catch her. What she quickly found was that although Jasper had no iron, salt, or glass, he did have a fat tom-cat who enjoyed chasing mice until they were too tired to run. The Witch spent two days hiding in the bristles of a broom while Tom lay sullen in front of it never sleeping and occasionally reaching out a paw to stir the dry bristles. Finally, the cat lost interest and the Witch made a run for it. Once she was out of the house, she turned into a fox and glared at the cat through the glass. He only yawned and stretched with an attitude as infuriating as his master's.

As it was, even having spent three days in Jasper's house, albeit in a broom, the Witch had learned nothing incriminating or of use in any way. There was only one thing in the Witch's opinion to be done. She would confront Jasper himself in the woods and make an end of him. She knew that Jasper made it a point to hunt under the full moon when the light was best. A Harvest Moon was nearing and the Witch thought full certain that Jasper would be out and about with not even a dog as company. Though he enjoyed the company of others, he hunted alone and that was just fine by the Witch. The night of the Harvest Moon, she scurried off to the woods and climbed a high tree. She took off her skin and hung it on the highest branch thinking this would be short work. The wind was high and the air smelled like rain and the skin fluttered like a gruesome kite.

The Witch smiled and tucked the skin a little tighter into the branch. Then, with a bright little pop, she changed into a cougar and lay waiting in the crook of the tree until she saw a lantern, dimmed but still bright to her cat eyes, bobbing through the woods. She narrowed her eyes and waited. Sure enough there came Jasper, quiet to a man's ears, but loud as the trump of doom to a cat. Leaves crackled, twigs snapped, and his breath sounded like a bull's bellow to the cougar. She dug her claws into the knotty wood of the old white oak and waited until he was right underneath—then she jumped.

Jasper slammed to the ground when the Witch-cat hit him and his rifle went flying. The Witch scratched and bit, but Jasper was a big man in a bear skin coat and the Witch-cat, much as she dug and scratched, couldn't quite make purchase. Jasper punched her in the jaw, but being hooked as they were together, they both went sprawling down the hill and slid in the leaves and debris. It had been a rainy month and the cold and wet had made the leaves slippery as mud. Even the Witch-cat couldn't gain a purchase and found herself skidding tail over head down the side of the bluff with Jasper still wrapped in her claws. Sometime during their fight a storm had started to brew and before the Witch knew it the wind was whipping something fierce. She growled and pawed, but Jasper's big coat, tough as any bear's hide, thwarted her at every turn. She couldn't rightly tell what was coat and what was man and just when she thought she had a hurting blow, she ended up with a mouth full of old fur.

Obsessed as she was with the coat and the man himself, she didn't notice the wind or the fact that her skin had come untucked from the tree until she heard the stretch and snap of it as it tore loose and fell to the ground in a sodden heap. Jasper, who was no fool, ran and grabbed up the skin and held it high above his head one-handed. And before the Witch could even leap, he threw his bear skin coat on her and took off down the hill toward home. He ran as fast as his feet could carry him, too fast for a man his size, so fast he thought his heart would burst. He could hear the howls and hisses of the Witch-Cat on his heels.

When he reached the home, the moon was high in the sky so it looked almost day. He flung open the door, wadded up the skin, and threw it into the roaring fire. Wet as it was, it hissed and popped, but the fire was strong, feeding on hickory scraps and old pine logs since dawn. The Witch-cat, feeling her skin catch fire, scratch on the door and howled. But she couldn't get in and finally as the last shreds of skin turned to ember and then to ash, the scratching stopped. It was near dawn.

Jasper found his door gouged nearly through in five places, but no Witch-cat was to be seen. Having lost her skin, the Witch had lost her voice, as well as her ability to change to another form. Bitter, she ran off into the woods. Folks wondered where she had gone, but some remembered that she had mentioned kin in far off places from time to time, and others noted that she'd always been a strange one. Jasper said nothing, but he made sure that the Witch's critters were cared for and her fields kept baled. Her horse came to stay with him and produced a fine mule, snow white and too clever for her own good, that Jasper named Fortune.

As for the Witch, for years, she hunted Jasper without success, but, in time, she began to forget exactly why, as the cat thoughts and the Witch thoughts began to mingle. Often she would begin the night with a thought to hunt Jasper and end the night with a fat hare in her jaws. She found that being a cat was much simpler and often more satisfying than being a woman. There wasn't much to worry about other than the night's food and a warm place to lay your paws, and there was always the moon and the night and the chase to look forward to. But on nights of full moons and especially during the Harvest Moon the Witch-Cat felt a strange stirring for what she could almost remember. On those nights she would prowl and howl in a voice that was almost a woman's. On those nights, it's still best to stay indoors. If you hear a cry like a child's from the edge of the woods, best to ignore it; best to stay inside and bolt the door, and make sure you keep iron and salt close at hand. It's nights like those that the Witch-cat still roams, not quite satisfied, and looking to settle a score.

Chapter 24:
Golden

I have heard this story all my life, but I don't think I've even heard the ending.

Once there was a very rich man who loved fine things. He loved them not for their beauty or grace, or even because they impressed the folks around him. He loved to have them, keep them and know that they belonged only to him.

When he was a young man he had purchased thoroughbreds and watched them race. But racing was a dangerous business and once after a horse had gone lame, he closed his stables and moved the horses to one of his country houses where he could watch them run and roam without any risk.

He was one of the first men in the county to purchase an automobile, and it was fine thing—black and silver with headlights that flashed like a young woman's eyes. He spared no expense on the car or its driver and, for a time, he was happy riding around the countryside in his fine car. Children would run out to see it and he gave his driver leave to blow the horn whenever he felt the need. Folks scattered or stared when the car was driven through town, and horses shied and headed for the ditches. But soon enough, other cars appeared, not so fine, but others just the same. Sometimes he would meet them on the road and the drivers would honk and wave. He did not wave back. And once or twice his driver had to swerve on a narrow road when a truck lumbered toward them. In time, no children waved and no country folks stared. Cars were still rare, but you saw them then and again. The man continued to buy cars, but he seldom took them out. They sat, polished and prim, in the garage he had built for them just a rock's throw from his fine stables.

There were other things that caught his fancy – musical instruments and those that could play them, fine clothes, sword canes and pistols, rare books, and strange beasts and birds stuffed and mounted. He collected them all, each one fit for a museum and the joy of any collector. Other men envied him his wealth, his stately home, his cars and horses, and his exquisite collections. He had many men who called themselves his friend, but none that he considered one. They came to his parties and danced in his halls. They smoked his cigars and drank his whiskey and wine, and they commented that they had seen nothing better, nothing more unique, nothing quite so perfect as the things that occupied his life.

But when they were gone and the staff had finished tidying up and had retreated to their own parts of the house, he sat alone, smoked his cigars and drank his small-batch bourbon and was not content. What good, after all, were things with no one to admire them? What good were the Persian rugs, grand pianos and horsehair duvets without someone to walk among them and know what a fine place it was, and what a fine life they lived.

He decided he would take a wife and made the fact known to the entire county. Fine gentleman offered their daughters and nieces as suitable candidates, but he found all of them wanting. They were girls raised in luxury, and so he felt they could not appreciate things as keenly as he desired. They looked at a rare painted and compared it to another they had seen, not as fine. They heard a sonata and remarked that this season or the other the music had been rarer, and the company more refined. The woman that he was looking for would see things with fresh eyes and appreciate them as he no longer could, as his guests no longer did. She would walk through his garden and smell each perfect bloom, and wonder at the hedge mazes and topiary designs. She would pause at the fountain and marvel at the purity of the water, the craftsmanship of the statues, and the artful play of shadow and light. She would know that this was a

127

perfection that could not be surpassed and never look for anything finer.

Eventually, he found such a woman, a girl really. She worked in a sewing factory from dawn to dusk and though her face was dirty and her hands calloused, she had eyes as blue as a spring morning and skin as clear as fine porcelain. He married her after the banns had been called and all etiquette served in a ceremony that dazzled the county. His friends proclaimed her the loveliest bride that had ever walked down the aisle, and the ladies were struck dumb with jealousy. The girl was too star-struck even to speak her vows. She only nodded when the minister proclaimed them wed. After a whirlwind honeymoon in Paris, London, and Rome, they returned home and she was equally bedazzled by the stables and the gardens, the fountains and the aviary, the many rooms and staircases, and the wardrobes full of the most beautiful clothes she had ever seen. Though her husband was near forty years her senior, she thought he was the handsomest, most educated, and most urbane of gentlemen. Though he was not kind, he was not cruel and she was grateful for a roof that didn't leak, meals that were more than bread and beans, and a coat that was more than patches held together with thread. She made sure to cover her calloused hands with the finest of silk gloves and only to speak when she was sure that an answer of yes or no was possible. Sometimes she sat for hours in the garden, even in winter and rain, admiring the way the seasons changed the statues and the elements transmuted the plants. She could not decide in which season the garden was the loveliest and, since she was not allowed to leave the garden or the house, she had no others with which to compare them.

Still, she was pleased, more than pleased, and it seemed strange to her that her husband seemed never to be contented. Even when she praised a painting noticing some small artistry that had escaped her eye before, he seemed empty. She asked, more than once, if there was something she could do, but he only shook his head and went back to planning another ball, charity event, or project. He was never still and nothing seemed to be able to hold him.

Five years into their marriage, a hot air balloon came to town. It was a strange thing and fabulous. It floated heavy in the sky, ripe as a pumpkin, its skin made up of patches. Everyone in the county was agog and queued for a ride at a quarter a head. The girl, now a woman, begged to ride in the balloon but her husband looked at its patches, eyed its pilot's dirty hands and worn suit, and decided that the balloon was not worth their time. The girl was disappointed, of course, but said nothing. That night, though, she crept out with a four shiny quarters wrapped in a silk 'kerchief, and headed straight for the one boarding house in town. She begged an audience with the pilot and for four times his going rate, he agreed to take her up in the night sky.

It was like nothing she could've imaged. The autumn night air was crisp and smelled of burning leaves and chimney smoke. The night sky was black as the finest ink and the stars twinkled like a fistful of diamonds. The town, so dull in the day, became a faerie village by night and her own home, still lit with torches and lanterns, was a dazzling jewel, a fairytale castle set on a hill. She found that she was weeping when they set down. And when they pilot offered her his handkerchief, she waved it away. She wanted to weep. She had never felt such joy or sorrow. She would never, she knew, see anything so fine again.

The next day she walked around the gardens and noted that the crepe myrtle was hanging low and most of its blooms had fled. The roses, though rare, were dropping their petals, and the fine statues had bits of moss growing over small chips and imperfections. It didn't matter to her that they weren't perfect. They were home and she loved them each and every one. But she knew, now, that there were things so wondrous that to see them was like being woken from a spell.

129

The man knew there was something wrong, something changed about the girl, but he couldn't quite put his finger on it. In many ways, the girl was happier after that night, but she seemed to have lost her sense of wonder. She no longer had a childish delight in small perfect things like a sculpted marzipan rose or a piece of lace woven so tightly that it seemed a thing grown and not crafted with sweat and tears. In short, she reminded him of himself. That was fine, he thought, but it also made him sad; he felt somehow that it was his fault. He searched for something new to present her—a dress, a pair of gloves, a portrait, or an impossibly rare book, but nothing seemed to delight her as it once had. She smiled, of course, and thanked him and then she filed the gifts away in a trunk or drawer. The world was simply not so bright for her or him as it had once been. It was a pity, he thought, but perhaps inevitable.

He began to look for new hobbies that he could enjoy with fresh eyes, but they soon wore on him. Time was making him slower, his eyes less able to read the smallest print, and his palate less able to discern the slight, but significant difference in cigars and bourbon and wine. He still stopped to smell the roses, but they didn't seem as sweet. And he started to find himself furious at the world, at time, and at himself. The girl, for such he still called her though she'd been a woman for years, was still young. He envied her youth and sometimes hated for it, too. Her legs never ached after a long day, and he never caught her squinting to catch the glint of something on the horizon. It was not her fault, but youth, being the one thing he could never buy, seemed now the finest thing of all.

He had always been known as a man with a big laugh and a big temper. Now, his temper began to surface more than his laugh and his friends, once so eager to dance at his parties and drink his whiskey, began to avoid him. Angered one day that he could not open his wall safe, he slammed his fist into the cast iron door repeatedly. Ashamed, he hid his swelling fist and arm for days. But eventually the girl found him out and called his personal physician, who wasted no time in setting the hand and dousing him with tonics so foul that he could taste them for days. The setting did not take, though, and within a week, his hand and arm began to blacken—to the wrist, then the elbow, and then crept upwards. A surgeon was called to remove his arm three fingers above his elbow. It saved his life, but not his pride. The man sat morosely in bed for days, unwilling to even have the lattice thrown open, until one day the girl arrived with a gift.

When he lifted it from the box, it caught the fire and glinted like a prism. It was cold to the touch, but heated quickly against the skin and was carved in the perfect likeness of nature. Nay, an improvement on nature! There was no telling what she had paid to have it fashioned in such short time. The artisan must have worked day and night for a week to craft it. It was one-of-a-kind in all the world and wholly his—a golden arm. His golden arm.

Suddenly, the world seemed as it once had. People marveled at the arm and asked to touch it. All agreed that there was no finer carving, no brighter gold, no rarer expression of artistry. He had special suits made to complement its color and canes made that fitted into the hand as smooth as would a glove. He almost thought, on occasion, that he could feel his fingers sliding over the items he touched. He almost felt that the arm was a blessing, his destiny, and that finally he was not the beholder of what was fine, but something fine himself, a piece of art, a sculpture, a thing to be admired and envied.

The girl was pleased that he was pleased. Truth be told, he seldom noticed her as she went about the garden and the house. Time passed. There were garden parties in the spring, dances by torchlight in the summer, and events in the ballroom in winter and fall. As the years went by, the man became known less for his fine house, beautiful wife, and exquisite taste and more for his golden arm. Newcomers to town were told about its waterfall, prize-winning horses, and, of course, The man with the Golden Arm. No one considered a visit to town complete without at least a glimpse of the golden arm and the man that bore it. And the man began to associate the arm with all that was fine. It was beauty and adulation and glory. It was, simply, golden.

But the man was not young, and had not been for many years. Losing his arm had taken a toll on him. He found that he could not walk very far in the evenings and that he sometimes had to squint to read a favorite book. Music was not as vibrant as once it had been and he began to value the low percussion more than the light, sweet voice of the violin. The girl, he noticed, had a few fine lines below her eyes and her hair was not so bright as once it had been. Even the finery of his house and grounds were diminished. Time had made its mark on all things—except, of course, his golden arm, which was a bright and glorious as the first day it had been cast.

The end came quickly for the Man. Perhaps too quickly. In the last few days of December he was taken with a head cold and put to bed. After a week, he was no better and the physician was called. He prescribed rest, tonics, and warmth. The man lay bundled in his bed, his golden arm catching glints from the hearth fire, and dozed. He died, on December 30, at 2:00 a.m. Every clock in the house stopped, which saved the servants from stopping them, though they did dutifully cover every mirror. He was buried a week later in a fine mausoleum carved years before by his father's father and bearing the family name etched in marble above the entryway. The entire county mourned, and even the Governor was in attendance at the laying-in. Flowers and gifts were sent from three states away, and some said that the President himself wrote the widow by telegram to let her know of his admiration.

After a month or two, people mentioned him less often, and after that, not at all. The girl, who people now called the widow, kept to herself in her fine house and she was lonely. The man, in his final years, had not managed his money very well and one by one the servants were let go, the horses were sold, and the treasures that the man had secured were auctioned. The girl walked the halls alone with only a maid and a cook to attend her. She managed the garden herself, pruning the roses, raking the leaves, and gathering the apples, peaches, and persimmons in baskets that her maid took to market each week. In the winter, they gathered dead wood until none could be found. The girl traded a fine brooch she found for a cord of wood, though her maid cried and pleaded with her. Warm hands and feet, the girl said, were more valuable than marble and gold.

The managed well enough for a while, but after a few years, the houses was in need of repairs that the girl could not tend to herself. There was a leak in the roof on the eastern end, some of the stair railing had grown loose, and the dry-wall cellar had developed a slow leak. She hired a handyman with long, flowing golden hair who stayed throughout the winter and fixed what needed fixing. Though she asked him to stay on, he left in the spring, fondly enough. But she was again alone.

She thought of selling the house, but there were none in the county that could afford it, and though she had her maid she could scarce afford to keep it. Things grew worse the next autumn. The summer had been hard enough. She tried to keep to herself, but people have a way of knowing what you'd rather they didn't in a small town. Before long, people knew she was in a precarious situation, yet few offered to help, though they had danced in her ballroom often enough and enjoyed her hospitality when it was hers to offer. The wind, in September, was already cold with a promise of snow and her maid reported black wooly worms by the score in the garden, a sure sign of a fierce winter. The woman searched the house for something to sell, but everything of value was gone. All but one thing. The golden arm.

133

She knew the golden arm was in the mausoleum with the man and though she hated the thought of it, she really had little choice. There are decisions that you make on the eve of winter with others beholding to you that you'd never make for yourself. So, the woman wrapped herself in a sturdy cloak and went by night to the crypt. She opened it, and with a heavy heart removed the golden arm. It was sold for a fraction of the price she had paid to craft it to a man that asked few questions, but paid her enough to keep her and hers through many winters to come. With a little luck and a lot of ingenuity, the girl thought, it might keep her for a decade or more. By then, perhaps, the house could be sold or other arrangements could be made. In the evening, when the moon rose, her eyes always turned west. It was said that a woman willing to work could make a name for herself there. And she and her maid had talked many times of opening a small boarding house with a few rooms and a good kitchen.

The girl felt something she hadn't in a long time – hope. She allowed herself to dream of a new life. She was, in fact, dreaming of a small house with a warm fire and a yellow cat when she first heard the footsteps downstairs. She and her maid were in the habit of stoking the fire high in the upstairs bedroom and sleeping with the door well shut to keep the heat in. The rest of the house was silent and cold as the grave. It was an old house and prone to creaks and groans, but they knew every single one of them. This was something new.

Her maid woke first, and was sitting still and white-faced when the girl woke with a start. There was someone on the lower floor, moving furniture and opening drawers. She could hear them muttering. She went to the fireplace and picked up a poker and waited by the door. After a time, she could hear the intruder begin to climb the stairs and open each and every door down the hallway. Again, she heard a mutter and a murmur, but couldn't catch what it was that was being said. Unsure what to do, she waited, and as she did, she became less afraid and more angry. Who was in her house, rummaging through the rooms, and asking, "Where? Where? Where?" Finally, despite her maid's pleas she flung open the door, but there was no one there. She searched each room by lantern and found no one, and the next day, she and her maid found nothing missing, no windows or doors broken, in short, nothing at all. They began to think they had dreamed it all until the next full moon when the same thing happened again.

Each time the footsteps grew closer and closer to their door, but when the girl flung it open, no one was there and no sound was heard for the rest of the night. The maid was in near-hysterics, but would not leave. Instead, she bought three stout padlocks at the hardware store and installed them on the bedroom door after much cursing and gouging of wood. When the spirit, for spirit they now deemed it, returned on the next full moon, it rattled the door but did not come in. The three locks held.

But after three return visits, the girl decided it was enough. She sent her maid to her mother's house for the night, though she begged her mistress not to go. Then, the girl undid the locks and waited sitting on the end of the bed, iron in hand, for the ghost. It was well after midnight when he came. The full moon was high in the sky and the stars were crisp as they can be only in the dead of winter. The air was so cold, despite the fire, that her breath made tiny puffs in the air. When the door opened, her hand shook, though she kept her resolve and stood. There was her husband, her dead husband, glowing slightly in the dark. "Where?" he asked. When she did not reply, he asked again, more impatiently "Where?" And then again, "Where, where, where?"

The girl knew she should be afraid. She knew she should shiver and cower, but she wasn't not afraid at all. She found she was furious. Furious at being left in a ramshackle house that she couldn't afford even to sell. Furious at a man who thought more about paintings and houses and golden arms than he ever did about her.

"Where is *what*?" she screamed, though she knew the answer.

"Where..." the spirit said, "Where is... where is my golden arm?" He asked it again, and then another time, and then a time after that. Finally, the girl had enough.

"Where?" She pointed at the fire, "There is your golden arm." And then at the rick of wood, "And there is your golden arm." Then at the bed by the fire, "And there is your golden arm." And finally at the baby that lay in it, "And there is your golden arm!"

The ghost walked forward silently, no more substantial than the girl's breath on the air. He gazed at the fire and the wood and the bed and the newborn babe lying wide-eyed and silent by the fire. He looked at the sleeping child and his golden hair for a very long time and then he smiled. It seemed to him that the boy's hair was as fine and as golden as ever his arm had been. He looked at the girl and then he smiled and then he was gone.

The next day the maid returned and the next spring the house was sold. No mention was made to the buyers of the ghost. But the girl knew he would not return. He had found something finer than his golden arm and that was, she hoped, enough. It was, she knew, enough for her.

Chapter 25:
Them That Hunger

There was a woman that lived in the woods, all alone in a house that was tumbling down, little more than sticks and stones piled together and held tight with ivy and myrtle and grapevines. People feared and pitied her, but mostly just left her alone. She was lonely, old, and unloved. Some said she was a wise woman while others contended that she was a witch. She had a fat black cat named Hobbes and kept a clutch of guineas that lived high in the rafter and were as mean as any dog. She grew herbs and small crops in her garden, planting by the moon and harvesting by the almanac. She left milk out for the faeries and corn-leavings for the coons, and did no harm.

There were some in town that said she had a secret treasure, because it's the sort of things that men say when they're in their cups on a late night with nothing else to say. They said she could conjure spirits and ask them where hidden things lay.

One dark night with the wind howling, they spoke of such things in the local tavern—a dull place with a pot-bellied stove and dry goods on the back shelves. The tavern served a watery stew and an even weaker beer. In the corner, a man travelling through drank his pale beer and listened. He was a small, dark man who cast no shadow. So slight and plain was he that not a soul even noticed him in the corner. Not a soul noticed him when he rose to leave, or that he placed no coins on the table. Few even remarked when the door opened and the cool night air kissed their cheeks and coaxed sparks from the stove. But a shiver ran through every man there and the waitress, a sturdy country girl with straw-colored hair and hands as calloused as any man's, opened the fat stove and laid another log on the fire.

The old woman did know many secrets. Some would've been worth more than gold to the right person. But she had very little that would've brought much at a country fair. What she couldn't harvest from the woods and lake, she grew in her garden. She could read the moon and stars, the turn of the air, and the rise and fall of the seasons. She understood the hearts of beasts—both on two-feet and four, and she did no harm. But doing no harm will seldom bring you the same. And her woodscraft and kind heart did not stay the dark man's hand the night he came calling. He pushed open the window latch left braced against the cold and before the old woman could wake, he bashed her head in with a fire iron. There was none to witness, but the cat in the rafters who, in the way of cats, watched all and said nothing. No doubt, he would have lit out into the night once he saw his mistress was done for, to find himself a new home with another old woman who, a cat may hope, would prove longer lived.

The dark man searched the house from top to bottom, but found nothing. But then, of course, who would be foolish enough to leave a great treasure in their cupboard or potato bin? The gold must be hidden in the well, he thought, or the smokehouse. Maybe it was buried deep in the garden or dug into the wall there. There were many places to look—a winter's worth of places, he thought. And, truth be told, his life was a hard one. He slept, most times, in a hedge row or unattended barn. If he could steal a few coins, or if his luck at cards and cups was good, he might spend a night before a fire. But folks didn't like his looks. And, after a day or three, the innkeeper would always advise that he move on, coin or no. As he wrapped the old woman in a quilt and tumbled her down to the fruit cellar, he thought it would be nice to sleep in a feather bed and have a good fire. It would be nice to dine on sweet blackberry jam and smoked ham instead of withered apples and watery stew. It would be nice to stay, even if it was only for a winter. So, he shucked off his shoes, pulled a quilt from the wardrobe, after he had made sure the fire was good for the night, curled up in the old woman's bed—still warm from her sleep.

A corpse in the cellar was nothing to trouble such a man, but he found that his dreams, despite the warm bed and flickering fire, were not sweet. He dreamed that a creature of ash and smoke rose out of the fire and peered into his eyes. He dreamed it divided into two, then ten, then twenty, and then more. That it kept on dividing until its numbers covered the earth and the world was wrapped in smoke and there was nothing to be seen but eyes dark as coal and bitter as blood. Eyes that stared and stared and stared. Eyes as flat and dark as mirrors cast in jet.

Nothing truly wild should ever be tamed. That's true of any creature, but even more so the raccoons. The old woman had known that, and yet, over the years she found herself talking to the creatures in the woods. Her cat, she never worried about. He was a cat and so could not be tamed. Though she called him Hobbes, she might was well have called him Dinner! Or Off the Table! Or What a Fine Cat! He came when he wanted and he left when he was done with her. She knew when he sat and purred it was for his own comfort and not her own. She talked to him and, he sometimes listened, in the way that a mother listened to a child babbling. There was a fondness in his listening and a sort of sly humor as though he believed she has learned a fine, but useless trick.

The raccoons, on the other hand, really listened. At first, they had crept up to the house and grabbed the corn-leavings with their hands slinking to the shadows to examine them and then eat. But in time, they came up in twos and fours and in covens of eight and twelve and twenty. Whole families of raccoons would sit and eat while she tossed them corn and apples and bits of dried meat from the porch. The kits were bold enough to climb the porch rails and chitter on the roof when they were in the mood for a snack. Some would even creep up to the edge of her skirts and look shyly at her with their ringed eyes, until their nerve broke and they went running back to their mothers.

She never meant to do it, but in time, she named them all. A name is a dangerous thing. A thing of power. It ties you to a place and a time. It defines you and in small ways changes you into the creature that's being named. Raccoons don't care for names. Most critters don't. They are and that's enough. But suddenly they found names like Bandit and Mischief and Smoke falling over them like blankets tying them to a way of thinking that wasn't their own. And the worst part of all was that in time they didn't mind. They begin to think of themselves not as part of the group or even a raccoon alone, but as Bandit and Smoke and Clever. It was a terrible and wonderful thing, they thought, as they sat in the dusk eating dried apples and listening to the old woman speak to them.

They had become a part of a place and time. They had become a part of her. And mostly, they were glad of it. They came, each night, for the words, as much as for the apples and bits of candied yams. They found as they slept and hunted and fished that they were hungry for them. That the old woman had woken in them an old desire and they began to think not just thoughts of the wild, but the thoughts of man as well.

Raccoons are curious creatures bound by no laws. Lords of mischief and moonlight, they follow their own minds. A great hunger lives inside every raccoon. A hunger for many things. And in their coal-black eyes you can see a reflection of yourself. In legend the raccoon is known as a trickster and a thief, but also said to have a kind heart. But there are others who believe it will be a raccoon, and not a wolf that devours the world. Perhaps it's true. A cat will run when it has no chance of winning. A dog will stay for love or pride. But a raccoon will stay because he knows he cannot lose. He knows that death means nothing to him.

They say that raccoons were formed from smoke and ash. Coal marks them with rings and a mask. They are born of fire and yet water, earth, and air hold no terror for them. They have mastered their fears and become the masters of earth and shadows and the places that lie between. They know the secret paths that men have long forgotten and that they only remember in their darkest dreams. It is said a raccoon can slip out of his skin as easily as a lady out of a fine silk dress, and that his spirit can go roaming as it pleases. Who knows what a spirit abroad may see or learn? But it can be sure that a raccoon knows man's heart as well, maybe even better than his own.

Animals know hunger and loneliness and fear. They know hate and despair and love. They know all the emotions of man and rise above them—except for the raccoon. The darkness that lies in a man's heart the raccoon knows all too well. He plays on it like a fellow may play a fiddle. But should his heart be won, he's more loyal than any hound. Raccoons have long memories. And like shadows in the evening, they are there, but unseen, slipping through the edges of things and watching all their rights and wrongs like guardian angels or avenging demons.

One raccoon, in particular, took notice of the dark man as he slunk up to the old woman's door and peered in her dark-paned window. Like all the raccoons, he had been given a name, and a title, as well. He was now King and he had come to think of himself as such. He was an old coon with a wide back and gray in his muzzle. He weighed near to forty pounds, and when standing was a tall as a good-sized toddler. He liked to stand, as it were, head and shoulders above the others in his clan. And the first sight the man saw when he woke and looked out the window was King standing in the garden, bold as brass, with the morning mist still laying low over the stubble. It was cold and the frost had slung little crystal spinnerets between the broken cornstalks and spent bean stalks. In the gray of dawn he looked as much spirit as beast, and the dark man felt a shudder run down his spine. He looked away to check the fire and when he looked back, King was gone.

But throughout the day he felt he was being watched. It was the same sly feeling of dread that had crept along his spine last night. It didn't come from any direction, it surrounded him. It whispered in his ear, it blew cold wind down the chimney, it rattled like dry leaves caught in a shutter, it slide like smoke through his thoughts. And sometimes he thought he saw something—like a shadow—creep out of a corner and stare. He told himself it was rats. Rats come in for the winter. Rats crept up from the fruit cellar. He boarded the cellar door tighter and stuffed rags in the windows and under the door. He built the fire high. But he still heard them, saw them.

Each day the man searched the garden and grounds searching for the treasure. He dug holes and sent weights down the well. He pulled loose stones from the chimney and rock wall and panned the creek looking for sunken chests or cubbies hidden in the bank. All the while he could feel himself being watched. He laid it down to paranoia, and guilt, maybe, though he had not thought himself a man to be troubled by such things before. He took to slinking about the place like a cat, looking left and right, and keeping his back to the wall. At dusk, he bolted the shutters and the door and stoked the fire high. He closed his eyes and covered his head with a quilt and did not rise until dawn. But he could still hear them scratching. He could hear the shutters and door rattle, he heard the plink of tiny stones and bits of dirt thrown down the chimney to weaken the fire. He could hear low voices, chittering back and forth throughout the night. Sometimes, he thought, he could understand one, a high voice, almost like a child's, that spoke in words that a man could understand. On the nights that he heard that voice, he buried his head between two down pillows and wept and shivered and shook. He prayed for dawn even though he knew there was no god who would hear his prayers.

Days turned to weeks and the weather grew so cold the dark man didn't left off his search for gold. The days were short and the dark came fast and with it came the voice and the shadows. The dark man began to think that maybe the old woman had killed him with the poker and tumbled him down the stairs, and that this was his hell. He reckoned that the voices he heard were the moans of the damned and the gray shapes the spirits of the lost. And then, one day, there was a knock at the door. Not a scratching, but a knock, at the center of the door.

It was well after midnight and the moon was full and high. The small man peered between the gaps in the shutter, but he could see nothing. The knocking continued, but the small man did not answer. He hid in the bed too afraid even to move when the fire burnt out, too afraid to reach for another quilt, too afraid to do anything but listen to the knocking that lasted throughout the night and stopped, it seemed, with the first light of dawn.

The small man slept through the day and when he woke in the evening he laughed. It was a dream, of course, a stupid dark dream brought on by ill humors and the cold. Everyone knew that the winter was a desperate time of year when the bones of the earth dredged up bad memories and worse truths. A wise man kept to himself and waited until spring. But when the night came, so did the knocking. And the small man found that it was more than he could bear. He barred the door with a chest of drawers and piled a week's supply of logs on the fire. He hid in the corner with a quilt wrapped around his shoulders and his hands over his eyes. It seemed to him that the knocking went on forever and that it echoed from every corner of the house and, from time to time, he thought he could see shadows, like smoke, flitting in the corners of the room. He wept and prayed and was alone in the black.

Perhaps a man would've taken pity on him. Perhaps a man would've seen true repentance in his eyes or weakened at his cries. But King and his kin were not men. They understood men, their kindness and cruelty, but they did not share a man's sentimentality. Like children, their hearts were just and cruel. Kindness, in their world, was repaid with kindness. And blood could only be repaid in kind. They understood they were driving the small man mad, and it was of little consequence. The minute he had touched the old woman's door, his fate had been sealed. King was the agent of that fate. He did not set the rules. They had been laid down at the founding of the earth. Blood must have blood.

The winter solstice is a time of power. Even the simplest of men feel a lighting of their hearts as the shortest day of the year passes. The last day of winter is laden with dread and hope. That's why folks in ancient times kept fires burning throughout the night—to make sure that the sun had a trail to follow, to make sure that the longest night wasn't an endless one. As the days in December darkened and slid toward Solstice, the little man skittered through the nights as best he could. He seldom ate and he spent most of his time wrapped in blankets by the fire with an eye toward the door. He left the house to bring in logs from the woodpile and, when it ran low, to pick up windfall limbs at the edge of the woods—but only when the sun was highest and never without the poker in his hand and his eye on the open door. The weight of the iron comforted him. Not that it mattered. Even at the height of day, he could feel their dark eyes on him. He felt them even in his sleep and he heard them in his dreams.

One night as he lay curled by the fire like a dog, the poker clenched in his hand, and a pillow braced over his head to block the sound of knocks and scratches at the door, a plan came to him. He remembered his grandmother had talked of days of power and the changing of the seasons with awe. She'd said he'd meet a bad end, too. He'd scoffed at her, at the time, but now he could see that she had been a woman of foresight. Maybe she'd known he'd meet this moment, alone, in the dark.

144

Maybe if he'd listened to her more closely, he wouldn't have taken the roads that led to this cabin. But, he had, and there was nothing to be done for it, but to make amends as best he could.

He waited until the morning of the Solstice to open the fruit cellar. It was no easy work. The cold had sealed the wood and iron to the floor. Weak as he was from hunger and sleepless nights, it took all his strength to pull the door open. It was black as the bottom of a well inside and he could smell the low, heady scent of earth and stone. The old woman, when he found her, was frozen solid, still wrapped in the blanket he'd tied around her when he tossed her down the stairs. Mice had nibbled her toes and fingers. Otherwise, she seemed in good repair. But light as she was, it took him more than an hour to carry her up the stairs. He found he was shaking as he went. Terrified that the gesture wouldn't be enough to sate them, and equally terrified that it would be.

When he had her in the light, he saw that her eyes were closed and that gave him a start. In his life, he'd made acquaintance of more than a few dead folks. And, it was his experience, that they usually kept their eyes wide and staring. Finding her with closed eyes and a smile on her face was more than upsetting. It confirmed what he believed for some time— that there were forces at work in this place that were beyond the kin of a regular man. But, in the end, there was nothing for it. Even a mouse in a cat's jaw struggles—not because he has any hope of escape, but because it's the nature of life. And hopeless and wretched as the small man was, he didn't want to die. He knew, from his own experience, that life was a hard thing and likely as not to end bitterly. Still, he reckoned he'd rather be wretched in the light than alone in the dark. That was it, in the end, the dark. What waited beyond it, no man knew, but it was an eternal enemy—a thing to be pushed against.

So he sat with the old woman at his feet, waiting for the turn of the day. And, when dusk came he opened the door to find them waiting, as he knew he would. He couldn't rightly say what they were. He would not have called them men or beasts. They had assumed the names they were called, as best they could, becoming Smoke and Bandits, Mischief and Jokers. They had winded themselves in smoke and night so that only their eyes could be clearly seen—a greater blackness against the very dark, like bits of fiery coal set against a midnight sky. The small man shuddered and picked up the woman's body and walked out into the living night. They formed around him like a living forest, closing behind him as a wall of night set with the stars that were their eyes. Beyond him stood the King, ringed in smoke, crowned with soot, his eyes blazing like twin suns.

The small man found it was hard to walk. That the very act of putting one foot in front of the other was at war with his very being. But he managed to do it, somehow, and to reach the night lord that stood before him. He half knelt, half fell at his feet, setting down the old woman in her blanket. He couldn't bring himself to raise his head. Instead, he crouched shivering and grimacing, waiting for judgment. But none came. The shadows neither spoke nor moved. They stood as a wall of darkness against the full moon, wreathed in mist, and utterly silent. The small man wept and pleaded, he reached out to them, and threw himself half-moaning on the body. But there was only darkness and shadow, moonlight and silence. What it meant the small man couldn't fathom. He had expected violence and despair. He had opened the door expecting horror, but, instead, he was met eyes burning like fire and a dark waiting. They bore into him until they were all he could see. Two fires consuming him, drinking him down like a fine whiskey, and leaving smoke and ash in their wake.

Whether he waited an hour or a day or a month, he never knew. It seemed as though time had no meaning, but when the men found him, crouched and ashen, rocking and wailing, his hair torn and his face gouged with scratches, he was grateful. They put him in ropes and then in chains and finally in a cell

146

with iron bars, and he was thankful for that as well. When he asked about the old woman, the jailer looked at him strangely and said she was fine and wasn't it a mercy they had gotten there in time before he could work any mischief, villain that he was. When he asked about the King of Shadows, the jailer said that he must be mad—the only King was across the water and no business of any honest man hereabouts.

Later, before other men with white jackets and kinder words came to take him away, the jailer told him how they had found him screaming at the door of the cabin, dragging an old sack, weeping, covered in dirt and ash, and pulling at his hair. He told the small man how they had heard him all the way at the pub and how the old woman had barred her door at the sound of him and that they had to carry lanterns to find him even with the full moon. The night had been so filled with mist that it had taken them an hour to find the cabin and only then because of the racket he was making. It was as if a cloud had descended to the earth and they were walking in the midst of it.

The jailer told him all this with a straight face, but the small man knew it was a lie. He knew it because at night, even though the jail door was barred and he was locked in his cell, he could hear them. He could hear them scratching and sometimes when he was very, very still he could see them, creatures of smoke and fire darting at the corner of his vision. He told the men who came to take him to a safe and quiet place that he would never be safe or quiet, but they only gave him a shot and told him that he was very ill. They put him in a soft room with walls the color of smoke and every night he'd see their eyes bright against the walls watching him. Sometimes, he thought, maybe it was he that was smoke and ash and fire and that all the rest of the world was very far away. He dreamed of cool nights and running in the dark, but woke to dull walls and a window too high reach. And every night he wept and prayed for iron and water and peace. But he never found them.

147

Chapter 26:
The Hungry Earth

Kentucky breeds three things—bourbon, horses and caves. It's the lime-rich soil that feeds the bluegrass and in turn creates thoroughbreds with bones like iron and hearts of fire. It's the mineral rich waters that help craft bourbons that twist and sing like smoke kissed with caramel and honey. And it's the caves running beneath the lime that are the hidden soul of the region.

This is a dark country with a long memory. The people who settled it were Irish, Scottish and later German. They recognized the haunted hills and stones of Kentucky and Tennessee and the Carolinas that were so like the landscape of their homelands. It was not an easy place. Each spring's tilling turns up a crop of new stones. Small bitter rocks like to shatter a plow, and flinty stones that crumble like ash under your fingers. The soil is a mixture of clay and loam. Wells dug yield sulfur as often as clean water. This is cave country. And beneath the red soil lie the bones and blood of the earth. You'll see hex signs on barns and wards like iron and salt are handed down man to man over the generations. When the soil is your life, you learn to read the whisper of the wind, the size of an oak leaf, and the meaning in an early frost. You watch the birds and the moon. You listen to the rhythm of the hollow earth.

The earth has stories to tell and they don't have happy endings. They are stories of blood and hunger. They are stories of despair. There are ghosts that walk the long corridors of the hollow earth—lost spirits, brokenhearted lovers, and those who came to love the dark earth and never left it.

There's a tale that says one of Mammoth Cave's first surveyors and guides, Stephen Bishop, can still be seen walking the dark corridors of the cavern that he loved and that, on occasion, he still shines a light to lead out those who have lost their way. But there are also those the hungry earth takes.

Caves have been discovered in most of the charted world and under the sea. But the South can boast both the deepest cave, Voronya in Georgia, and the cave system of the greatest length, Mammoth Cave. As it name implies, Mammoth stretches like a river beneath the state covering 390 miles. It is not lonely, it is surrounding by a sea of smaller caves and cave systems boasting names like Onyx, Crystal, Lost River, and, of course, Sand Cave. For the past millennia, men have used caves for shelter and storage. They have been homes, sacred places, and tombs. Pirates and outlaws have sheltered in them and moonshiners have used to store and make their illicit wares. They are places of mystery and deep silence. They hold secrets they are not willing to share standing as silent sentinels in the dark earth, their stalagmites evidence of the slow march of time they have endured.

In the early 1900s, the area around Mammoth Cave, lovingly known as Cave City, was in the middle of a cave war. The finding of a cave was a money-making opportunity—if it was the right sort of cave, and there are many sorts of caves as there are men. There are low caves not fit for a grown-man to crawl through, dank caves with weeping walls and floors so slick that a man has to brace himself with each step, and sandy-floored caves with roots twisting through their ceilings and walls that put you in mind of being in an old root cellar. Caves these are, but for the purposes of a cave-finder, they were of little use. What you wanted was a large cave—but not too large—with high walls and a ceiling covered with twisting formations, stalagmites and stalactites aplenty, and hints of crystal and fool's gold in the stones. The cave you were looking for should be cool, but not too cold, and dry and sound. Tourists don't like to worry about slipping or to smell the low rot of old waters and the plants and fungus that shun the sun. Visitors like a nice cave dark enough for a good scare, but not too dark to see their sweetheart's face. They like round geodes they can take home as souvenirs, shiny crystals, and shards of stone shot through with mineral lacing. In short, they like a bit of a scare in relative safety and for about the same price they'd pay for a ticket to a picture show.

There was no shortage of men in Kentucky who made their trade by finding caves. They studied the signs and hunted the hollow earth like it was a beast. A farmer who found a nice cave on his own property might use it for storage or to hide a still. But a clever man would rent it out to a fellow with entrepreneurial spirit who'd show the locals and visitors alike through the darkness for a price of two bits. If the fellow was a showman, he might get a bit more, especially if he threw in a ghost story or two and maybe a legend about a weeping woman or a lost soldier.

Given the right circumstances, a cave could be a source of income for years to come. It required little to no upkeep and the visitors just kept coming. The automobile saw to it. The first thing that people wanted to do once they could travel was to see what lay beyond a day's ride on wagon or horseback. A man could get across state on a tank of gas. A real adventurer might make a road trip lasting a weekend, and a man of means might make a summer of it. Attractions like Niagara Falls, the Grand Canyon, and the Great Lakes filled men's minds. Natural beauty was an inspiration, a gift straight from the hand of God, and caves were all of that plus a thing of mystery. Exploring the heart of the earth, even if it was only for a half hour, seemed as mysterious and romantic as a voyage at sea or a trip to the stars. This was a forbidden country—a place men weren't meant to see. So, of course, they wanted to see it.

Floyd Collins and his brother, Homer were cave finders and showmen. They were pirates on the hollow sea searching for a treasure worth more than gold. In a few years, they had made quite a name for themselves finding caves of moderate size throughout Kentucky. But, after the discovery of

Mammoth Cave, they set their eyes of bigger game. Finding a small cave tucked under some farmland had been fine, but there was no glamour in it. There were many who suspected, Floyd and his brother included, that Mammoth Cave was the beating heart of the hollow earth and that all caves in the area were tributaries to its dark ocean. Finding those tributaries was a problem though as many caves, especially the smaller ones, became impossible to navigate at a certain point. There was no sonar in those days, no way to explore a cave other than step-by-step lantern in hand. It was dangerous work and exciting. You were alone in the dark even with a man at your side. There was no greater test of your own fortitude and skill than exploring a new cave, mapping its passages, and then turning it to your hand. Most men worked in teams, but the most daring, and some might say the most reckless, worked alone.

In 1917 Floyd Collins discovered Crystal Cave, a cave of remarkable beauty whose only detraction was its remote location. Tourists wanted a cave was near a thoroughfare, lodgings, and hopefully a nice place to eat. With that in mind, Floyd decided to scout out a location along the highway leading to Mammoth Cave. The area, after all, was riddled with limestone and potential caves could be under almost every farmstead just waiting for discovery. Floyd made a deal with three local farmers whose land lay along the path to Mammoth. If he found a cave (or two or three) on their property, he'd split the potential profits with them. Neither they nor Floyd were disappointed. Floyd's sense for finding caves was as keen as his business sense and within a few weeks' time Floyd discovered and enlarged a hole into a larger cave that would come to be known as Sand Cave.

For the next eight years, Floyd worked to explore and enlarge Sand Cave. Despite the danger, Floyd preferred to work alone. He told his family that he had found a large cavern within Sand Cave that, he hoped might connect with other cave systems—maybe even with Mammoth Cave itself. On a cold day at the end of January, Floyd was exploring Sand Cave when he ran out of lantern oil. Maybe it was the excitement of finding a new passage or his narrow focus on his work, but before he knew it, he was in the dark. And, though he knew the cave well, he was in passages that he had just begun to chart. On his way out of the cave, a large rock crashed from the ceiling and pinned Floyd's leg to the floor. His efforts to move the rock failed. And, though he was quickly missed, no one had any luck removing the rock or Floyd from the cave. His friends brought down food and ran an electric light to provide some warmth, but they could do nothing to remove the stone. Floyd was only 150 feet from the entrance.

After a week, the cave passage Floyd's friends were using to reach him collapsed in two places. Unable to reach him and fearing other cave-ins, rescuers began digging a shaft to reach Floyd. But they did not reach him in time. Floyd Collins died on February 13, four days before dig teams were able to reach him. The stone that had killed him refused to be moved. So, Floyd's friends and family solemnly filled the shaft with earth making the most famous cave Floyd had discovered his tomb. For although Sand Cave had never taken off as a tourist destination, Floyd's plight had touched the heart of the nation. People travelled from around the country to watch the rescue efforts and lend a hand. A debutante in New York sent her personal physician to give advice and offer support to Floyd, and others came simply to offer moral support. Floyd himself was cheerful throughout the ordeal, even giving an interview while he was trapped. Interest in his story brought even more visitors to the area and made Mammoth and Sand Cave household words.

Two months after Floyd's burial, his brother Homer and a group of friends reopened the shaft and dug a tunnel on the opposite side of the cave passage where Floyd had been trapped. In the spring of 1925, they recovered his body and the next day he was buried on the Collins family farm, not far from

Crystal Cave. Floyd had been laid to rest, but it seemed he wasn't going to be allowed to rest in peace. Two years later, when the Collins family sold their farm and Crystal Cave, Floyd's body was removed and placed in Crystal Cave, now named Floyd Collins Crystal Cave, in a glass-topped coffin. Two years later, Floyd's body was stolen and returned weeks' later missing the injured leg. After that time, Floyd was moved deeper into the cave in a chained casket. He was not moved again until 1961 when Mammoth Cave National Park purchased Crystal Cave and closed it to the public. The Park Service reinterred Floyd with no little effort. It took fifteen men three days to remove his casket and tombstone from Crystal Cave. Some folks said that Floyd didn't want to go, and there were protests from cavers who felt that Floyd should be allowed to rest in one of the caves he discovered.

In the end, Floyd's legacy was probably more than he could've hoped for. His plight created interest in the Mammoth Cave area and eventually led to the creation of Mammoth Cave National Park. His life has inspired several books and even a musical, and later expeditions confirmed that parts of Mammoth Cave do actually run under Sand Cave. Although no passage between the two has yet been discovered, Sand Cave is officially a part of Mammoth Cave National Park. And, Floyd Collins will always be remembered. His tombstone names him as one of the world's pioneers in cave exploration. Whether he walks the passages of Sand Cave looking for that elusive passage is hard to say. Sand Cave was closed to the public in the 1960s. So, if Floyd walks there, he walks alone the footsteps of the visitors to Mammoth Cave echoing above him.

Chapter 27:
Roots

Granny says it's just a root cellar and there's no reason to be afraid. That the only things down there are canned fruits, winter apples, and potatoes cut in pieces for their eyes. She says the smell is from the earth walls and ceiling, and that's it's just the moist air trapped in a small space. But there are dead things in the dark—spiders curled in tight fists, fat beetles with broken shells, mice with their little eyes gone white, and worse things—things that don't have names. And they are hungry. They take the spiders and beetles and bottle flies and mice, but I can feel them nibbling at me when I climb down the ladder into the dark. I can feel them tasting me, trying to determine whether they could tumble me down to the earth floor and eat me bit by bit like all the others.

They don't like it here. Maybe they don't like it anywhere. I can feel their little cold sighs on my ankles and cheeks in the dark and I fumble to light the lantern. I can feel their dark little eyes boring into me, wondering what I am, a kind of creature who comes and goes from the dark. Things that come down to the dark don't leave, except for me. I come down to fetch apples and blackberry jam and hanging garlic and then climb back into the light while they sit and sulk in the dark and plan. Theirs is an old darkness and a bitter one. They remember a world where the nights were longer and the winters colder. They remember people huddled by fires fearfully hoping for dawn. They remember when folks whispered their names and made the sign of the fox to keep them at bay. Now, folks just flick an electric light and they're relegated to the shadows behind the curtains, the pool of dark at the base of a bed, or the depths of the closet. Except for here. There are no electric lights in the cellar and a flashlight just won't cut it. But a good kerosene lantern with the wick set just right will light the cellar from ladder to drying rack. The trick is lighting it.

It's always a race. Will I be able to get down the ladder, grab the lantern, and flick the match quick enough or will they be able to drag me down? Folks say I'm quick. I won the half-mile dash first place this year and second the year before. But they're old and sly and they know that sometimes waiting for the opportune moment is just as important as the action itself. And there's something else, too. They know that I'm their very last chance. Granny never comes into the root cellar anymore. It's too hard for her to go up and down the ladder, and Dad has talked about putting in a dry goods pantry in the back of the house or maybe a standing greenhouse with a place for hanging herbs and preserves. If that happens, then the cellar door will be nailed flat shut and they'll have to make do with moths and spiders and whatever other small fare they can coax in from the dark. Most critters steer clear of this place, even though they could get in with a little burrowing. But it's better to be cold and take your chances in the night than to be down here with them.

Time's running short, and who knows what will happen when there are only spiders and millets and fleas. Maybe they'll curl up like the little mouse in the corner. It's the mice that always make me mad with their sweet little hands and tiny pink noses. I open up the vent on the lantern and let it flare for the mouse. The airs warms a bit and the shadows pull up tight against the walls. I pick up a winter apple and take a bite and I wonder if the mouse did the same. I hope so. I hope that he had some sweetness before they pounced—cruel as any cat. I pick up the apricot preserves and tomato relish and put it in the bag I brought with me. Then I walk back over to the ladder, set the lantern down, and blow it out. I'm at the top slamming the cellar door before they even get halfway across the floor. Then I throw the iron latch and listen. I can feel their despair and I'm glad enough.

155

I don't have a name to call them, although I'm sure there are some that know it. But I hate them just the same. Mouse-killers, smashers of beetles, stealers of hope. They wither the apples and blacken the preserves when they can and they make the walls grow gray with mold. They're all the bad things that live in your dreams and want to ooze out into the light. Only they can't. They live in the dark places in the world, in the shadows under your bed, in the places the streetlight doesn't reach, and in your dreams. They aren't strong enough to come into the light.

But even a soulless thing lurking in shadows can hope. That's how I know they'll never curl up and sleep. That's how I know the next time I pull open the root cellar door they'll be waiting. Because waiting is what they do, and there's always hope that a great darkness is coming—an endless night—when the Sun takes its final breath or the sky grows dark with ash. That's when they'll be free. But, for now, they live in the root cellar, bound by iron and willow, alone and whispering in the dark, held in check by a little girl's hand.

Chapter 28:
Strays

Sometimes kindness is its own reward.

She could see them on the edge of the woods, crouched low in the brush, hungry and afraid, but hopeful. New ones. The regular ones, the ones that came around every night, were already at the foot of the garden. Waiting for her to put the food into bowls and close the door. A few were bold enough, these days, to come almost within reach of her broom. They knew her. She took care of them. They were still afraid.

It was her kind, mostly, that hurt them. But the elements and animals, predators like foxes and cougars and even wild dogs, took their toll. They were so small. They weren't fast or strong. Some of them didn't learn quickly enough. They remembered, somewhere in the back of their minds, that people had taken care of them. They had petted and doted on them, bought them ribbons and treats, and gave them soft places to sleep. They hadn't had to worry. They hadn't had to hide. But that wasn't true anymore.

There were bad people. People trapped them. They hurt them. Sometimes they killed them. Sometimes they did it because they were afraid. They thought they carried disease or that they might attack. They didn't want their yards or houses upset. They didn't like the smell. They didn't like to think about them. Sometimes, though, they hurt them for fun. They hurt them to laugh and to watch them die.

Those that escaped started to learn. They kept to the shadows in the day. They hunted when they could in the woods. But mostly they came here at night. They wanted and they hoped. This wasn't home. There was no more home. There could never be. But this was safe, for a while, and there was food, and there were more of them. They were safer when there were more of them. No one could catch them all. And then there the old woman—she called them by names she made up, and she remembered to call them the same names, as if they were worth something. She helped them when she could, and when they couldn't go on, she helped them then, too. Maybe it wasn't much, but it was something, so they came every night, in twos and threes. They crept up to the door or the garden path, or the edge of the woods and they waited.

Sometimes bad things came here, but they drove them off. They couldn't kill them, but they were many. Too many to be stopped by any one or two. Too many for a cougar or a dog pack, even. She taught them that. They had strength. They knew by her smell that she was old, because they lived in a world where there was nothing but scent, where all you were and are and were planning was as clear as taking a breath. They knew one day she would not come to the door and then they would be alone. But they hoped. They hoped that when the day came she might join them. They thought that might be true. That there were things beyond life and death, and that even in death they might have something of her. A spirit. A hope. Or something more. She sang to them sometimes. Songs they remembered. They knew them from times before. Sometimes they sang back—tried to, anyway. It was hard to remember and they couldn't make the sounds right. She knew they tried. That counted for something. Tonight was different, though.

Tonight there was something more on the wind that the old woman or the food or their brothers and sisters. Somewhere along the line they had become more than ones and twos and fours and twenty. They had become one and there was a sort of synthesis to their thought. They thought in the now and then they did. Others joined the colony and some faded away. But they were thought and action. There were people here. Maybe bad people. They were not so close, but not so far away. They smelled like metal and smoke and blood and hate. They smelled like death. They knew death. It came at you with guns and wire. It was food that burned and cars that ran you down. It was fire and drowning. It was always waiting and behind it there were men with smiles that smelled like blood. One man you could hide from. Two you could run from. More though. Many. They could scatter, but some would be caught. And they knew in their hearts that there was more at stake.

Death was coming for them. True. Always. But it was coming for her, too. How they knew this, they could not have said. It was in the air like electricity. Maybe it was something they learned in the shadows. Maybe it was what you had to learn to survive. That second or third sense that kept you moving, told you not to go beyond that yard, to touch that food, to stay low, stay safe. And they were right.

They heard the car, cars, truck, trucks. She heard it too and started. She dropped a bowl. They pulled back to the shadows. Laid low. But they did not scatter. The men were making words. Bad words. Hard words. One hit her across the breastbone with the end of his gun and she went down hard, on her knees. She was crying. She was crying for them and then men were laughing. What they were saying, they didn't know. Not the words, really, but they knew what they meant. They meant kill them. Kill them all. Kill them with blood and smoke and pain. Kill her too and burn the house down and then go home and go to sleep and get up tomorrow.

A buzz ran through them like fire. It was painful. It was what it felt like to hate. They never hated. They just were. They knew the taste of hate, though. They remembered it. Pain, fear, loss, hunger. Those were their words now. But she had taught them other words. She had taught them love and hope and faith. And now they had hate. They stood, all of them, and there were many. They didn't wait, they just came forward. There were too many of them. They were like an army. So many that the old woman couldn't count them. They never came out together, not even for her. They learned to share and wait. They learned to live in shadows. They were moving now in the light of the moon they were twenty and thirty and fifty. They were small. It was easy to hide. Who would count them? Who wanted to? And now the old woman was laughing and they smelled fear. They smelled fear on the men, and even though guns were firing, they were so many. So very many.

A man was yelling that you had to shoot them in the head, nothing else would work, and to not let them bite you, but no one was listening. There were just so many, wearing sneakers and sandals and dresses straight from Church. Some of them still had toys that they couldn't quite remember what to do with, but they knew they were important. They were to a child grubby and ragged. Some had bones showing through patches of skin. Others had patches of grave moss growing on their faces and arms. But they were smiling. All of them. Smiling with baby teeth and braces and righteous fury. And they were hungry. So. Very. Hungry. After all, they hadn't been fed tonight.

Chapter 29:
Fortunate

Deborah stands under the tree on the playground, the big oak, with the twisted branches. She's there every recess from the time the bell rings until it rings again, and she'll tell your fortune for a quarter. It has to be a quarter, not two dimes and a nickel, or twenty-five pennies. Only a quarter will do and it's always true. She said Billy would fall and break his arm in two places, and he did. We all heard it snap-snap when he jumped from the swings after the teachers told him to stop going so high. She said Sarah Michael would leave, and so she did. Her family moved off to Ohio after the fall break, but she sent us a postcard with a picture of a buckeye and a quarter taped to one side. Deborah sent her a message by mail, but she wouldn't tell what she wrote. Not even when I asked her twice. "There's selling and then telling," she said, "But what I wrote's not for sale. You can only have your own and no other." I'm not sure what that means, and I wish I did. I really do.

I've never asked for a fortune of my own. I have to admit that I'm scared to. They aren't like those cookies. They're not usually funny and sometimes not even nice. And once you know, you know. Billy knew his arm would break snap and snap again a full month before it happened. He knew it every day, but he still jumped out of the swing. He said he didn't care and that it was only words. He was right, but it still happened and now he has a cast with everyone's name written on it. He has to scratch his arm with a fork or a knife and it doesn't really work. He says it itches. It itches fierce and all the time.

It does, too. That's the best word for it. It itches. When I see Deborah standing in the shadow of the tree with a pocket full of quarters, I feel this itch. How many must she have? Does she keep them in a big jar like my Grandma's buttons, or take them in a bag to the Coinstar machine and turn them into dollars, or just give them away? Maybe it doesn't matter. Maybe she doesn't want them at all, but she has an itch, too. Maybe all those futures inside her build up like a bottle of Coke when you give it a shake. Maybe she has to let them out or else.

I must've kept that quarter in my pocket for a week. It was a found quarter, which some folks say are ill luck anyway. My Grandma always told me never to pick up found coins, you never know what they've been marked with—good luck or ill—but my Mama has always picked up every penny she could find and never had any bad luck because of it. Maybe it only works if you believe in it, like some people say curses do. I don't know. But I thought maybe a found quarter might cancel out any bad luck the fortune might have. I hoped it would anyway.

But even that hope didn't give me courage. I spent half of recess sitting on the swing spinning in a slow circle while the chain unwound and wound again. Indecisive is no way to be, but it's how I am most of the time. Sometimes I need a push to get me going and that's just what I got—from Billy Callahan no less. I was sitting there spinning and staring at Deborah hard enough to work a hole in the air when he shoved me clean out of my swing. I hit the clay with a thump and looked up scowling, but he already had my swing and was laughing like an idiot. I thought about ratting him out to the teacher, but as it was, I guess he did me a favor.

Well, maybe not a favor, but he pushed me in the direction I wanted to go. Sometimes even when you know something is bad for you, you have to have it—like that second piece of chocolate birthday cake. You know your stomach is going to ache something terrible, but you just can't stop yourself. After all, how often do you have a chance at birthday cake? I guess Deborah and her fortunes were the same. I had a feeling they would be bitter, but I still wanted a bite. My Granny always told me that curiosity killed the cat. I never saw any sense in that, since cats were quick and curious and as luck would have it, always seemed to end up at the right end of a transaction. I'd put my money down on a grizzled old Tom or a scrawny Molly against a dog or a fox any day of the week. Dogs worry about being respectable and foxes are full of pride. But cats are mostly full of meanness, hissing, and spitting. Even one sitting on your lap purring up a storm will turn on you and bite you just for the fun of it. That doesn't stop you from petting them though, does it?

So, I walked up to Deborah digging for the quarter in my pocket and held it out to her. She took it and shoved it in the pocket of her skirt with about twenty others just like it. There were days she jingled when she came in from recess. What she did with all those quarters I never knew. Maybe she threw them all in wishing wells and made some wishes for herself, or maybe she had an account down at the local BB&T and rolled the quarters up smart each Sunday and dropped them off on her way to school Monday morning. I never found out and I guess it didn't matter in the long run. What mattered was Deborah took my quarter and then stood looking up for a minute and then leaned forward and whispered in my ear. She whispered just five words. Five. There's a lot you can say in five words.

It wasn't a bad fortune or a good one. It just was. She didn't tell me I was going to break my arm or that I'd move away. Some might say it wasn't my fortune at all. But, then again, it was. Or maybe it was mine only because I was the one to make it happen. Who knows, really, how such things work. Is a room empty even if you don't look in it or is it the looking that makes it so? Maybe it's someone taking a peek that adds the emptiness. Maybe fortunes are the same way. They happen every day, but we don't know it unless we lay our quarters down.

I had to wait a long time. Two summers and a month passed. It was two days before school was about to start, those long, lazy August days when it still seems like summer, but you can taste fall in the wind. The trees know, though. You can see it in the way their leaves are starting to crisp up at the edges. Trees understand the meaning of time in a way I don't think we can. They know all about waiting. They just don't mind it. When the moment came, I wasn't afraid. I was standing at the crosswalk when I saw the doll's hat fly into the street. The little girl, no more than four or five, pulled loose from her mother's hand, her own hand outstretched for the hat caught on a breeze. The car seemed to move so slowly. Everything moved so slowly. But I remembered those five words and I wasn't afraid.

Later they wrote a story about me in the local paper and the mayor gave me an award and a savings bond worth $100. They took the little girl's picture too holding her doll wearing its hat. Her mother cried and shook my hand and then hugged me. She kept wiping her eyes with one hand. The other she kept on the little girl's shoulder. The little girl didn't say much at all. I could tell she was glad to have the doll's hat back, though. She kept adjusting it until it had just the right tilt, and I guess that's as good a thank you as anything.

I looked for Deborah in the school yard the first day of school, but she wasn't there. When I asked the teacher about it, she said she'd moved during the summer, but she gave me her address when I said I wanted to write her. It took me a week to work out the words and another to send the card, but in the end I did. It said simply: *The little girl was saved.* I didn't tape another quarter to the postcard. I guess I'm not as brave as Sarah Michael—or I wasn't that day anyway. You never know just how brave you are or aren't until the day comes.

It's been a year almost now and I haven't heard back from Deborah. I didn't think I would. But I keep my eye out for her. I can't say I'd want to know my fortune again, but then, you never know. I keep a quarter in my pocket, a found one, just in case. You never know, after all, when you'll need some change.

Chapter 30:
Found Things

We have forgotten so much. There's a reason that folks used to make bottle trees and hang witches' balls. There are spirits in the air and they are hungry. There are dark things that scratch at night trying to get in. Horseshoes aren't hung above doors for luck. They're hung by those who remember that iron and silver and salt guard against the dark. People used to know these things. They passed them down in front of log fires and cast iron stoves in the darkest days of winter. They stitched them into quilts and carved them into wood posts and lintels. They made sure they were remembered and part of remembering is telling.

But then came the electric light. Hydropower flowed over the South like kudzu and stories gave way to televisions, electric ranges replaced wood stoves, and fire places were boarded up to make way for baseboard heaters and central heat and air. Stories aren't creatures of the light. They thrive in the flicker of candles and the slow days of autumn and winter. Ideas pop like chestnuts on a hot flame when exposed to halogen bulbs and Wi-fi. Stories live on the page and in the rhythms of the human heart. Without them, we are helpless to defend against the shadow in the corner, the foxfire dancing on the split rail, or the hungry dead that walk deserted roads looking for things lost.

Faith is a curious thing. People have faith that a flashlight will help them find their way, that a floodlight will keep them safe, and that a night light will hold their nightmares at bay. But light is a fickle thing at best. Each light creates a shadow and in that shadow are the stuff of dreams and doubts. And with no way to tame those things that gibber and prance at the edge of our consciousness, we find ourselves alone in the dark with only a candle for a guide.

There a danger in found things. People used to know that it was ill luck to pick up a coin or a trinket found by the road. Luck could be sewn up in anything—in nail or horse shoes, in coins and hair ribbons. And there's more than one kind of luck.

Never give a witch a pin, the saying goes, or anything iron. A gift given has no power for good or ill over the receiver. But a thing found, a thing shining and fine lying by the side of the road, is a thing of danger. A coin can be so much more than a coin, a piece of candy more than a simple sweet, good luck and bad can be sewn side by side into an apron pocket and who's to say what either side means or what luck was really intended. The true intent that lurks in a man or woman's heart may not be what comes to his lips or even to his mind. How many well wishes are curses in disguise and how many found things are just waiting to be picked up? And sometimes you'll find what you're looking for whether you want it or not.

My cousin had a lucky coin. Lucky for him, but not for others. He picked it out of a wishing fountain on a dare even though everyone knows it's the worst kind of luck to take a coin out of a fountain—almost as bad as taking a flower off a grave. Every time he flipped it, it always came up what he said—heads or tails—take your pick. But, in the end, he put it in a soda machine by mistake. So, I guess there's some other fellow who's lucky at coin tosses. Maybe it ended up in a penny jar, or it's in another vending machine somewhere. Who knows?

As for me, I found an eraser. That doesn't sound very exciting and there would've been no reason to pick it up, but I really needed an eraser. The one on my pencil had snapped clean off the way they sometimes do and I knew we were having a pop quiz in algebra that day. We always had a pop quiz on Wednesday so it wasn't very "pop" at all. But, there it was, one of those erasers that fits on the end of your pencil

167

with just a little wear laying on the ground in front of my locker like someone left it there for me. So, I picked it up and put it in my pocket and, as luck turns out, I didn't even have to use it in class. Mr. Farris, our teacher, had called in sick and the sub was more interested in knitting than teaching us anything.

It was because of the sub that I found out what the eraser could do. If she'd be putting us through our numbers or made us watch another film strip, I might've forgotten about the eraser or lost it, or left it in my pocket so that it ended up getting washed and dried until it was just a nub. But, as it was, we had a whole class to read, listen to music, or do whatever we pleased as long as it was soundless and didn't interfere with the sub's stitchery. I found myself doodling, as I often do when my mind's on something else. In front of me Sarah Jefferies and Bill McCormick were making doe eyes at each other and trying to pass each other a note without getting caught. So, I drew their names with a heart on a piece of notebook paper and then a picture of them looking mooney-eyed. But it didn't turn out right, so I erased it. Then I drew a little house with smoke coming out the top and a bunch of flowers twined around each other so that the whole edge of the notebook was nothing but roses and tulips and lilies. I was coloring in a few of them when the bell rang and, since algebra was the last class of the day, I hustled off to my locker, threw my algebra book inside and made a dash for the bus. Our bus driver is not one to wait—leaving a couple of kids behind wouldn't leave her sleepless. I think, in fact, running a couple of kids over wouldn't leave her sleepless, either, but that's another story.

The next morning I heard that Sarah and Billy broke up. Just like that. They broke up right outside the classroom and Billy even missed his bus and Brad Williams had to give him a ride home. It was a bad scene, apparently, with screaming and crying in the hallway, so everyone had to repeat it about twenty times and half the class claimed to have been there. It was too bad, I thought, but really it happens all the time, so I didn't put two and two together. I've always been bad at math, so I guess that's no real wonder.

But after awhile things became more obvious. I'd been drawing a chain of lilies that didn't look quite right in English lit, so I erased the whole batch and started over with roses. Then, I drew Coach Hadley twirling his whistle like he does when he's bored, but I erased it and drew a basketball instead. I drew a lot of things and erased them that day. It was a rainy day and those tend to make me moody and prone to daydreaming. I wish to God it had been sunny because that day Coach Hadley lost his whistle and spent half the class complaining about it and all the day lilies outside the school died. They just curled up on themselves like little black stumps until there was nothing left at all. There were other things too—things I'd drawn, things I'd erased. An old barn burned to the ground that looked a good deal like the one I'd drawn, but hadn't liked the look of and half-erased before the last bell rang, and the flag pole outside the school snapped clean off after I drew and erased it. I'd been drawing a picture of the school and I finished it on the bus. Just to be safe. I was starting to get more than a little scared. But these things don't happen. Erasers don't erase real things. They just don't.

Except this one did. I wasn't sure. No, that's not true. I was sure, but I still needed to test it one more time, so I drew a picture of our mail box and then erased it that night. In the morning, it was knocked over and crushed—a victim of a midnight game of mailbox baseball. It wasn't the first time it had happened, but it wasn't a coincidence either. It was the eraser.

And that's the rub of it, no pun intended. What do you do when you find a lucky coin or a magic eraser? Sure, you could use it, but you never knew how things would turn out. Erase "Algebra" and maybe class is cancelled that day or maybe the school burns down or your teacher dies. Erase some a rain cloud and maybe a tornado comes to replace it—or maybe a sunny day. You just never knew. And, then, there's always the chance that you forget. Erasers look a lot alike. This one was pink—like about a million others, with a few black marks on the end. What if I mixed it up with another eraser? What if I dropped it and then someone picked it up, someone who erased say a picture of a cat or their house or their own name? A piece of magic is a wild thing. And, like any wild thing, it's as likely to bite you as to lick your hand. It can be bent to your will, maybe, but it can never be tamed.

I spent a lot of time thinking about what to do with the eraser. I thought about throwing it in the wood stove or even putting it back where I'd found it. But, in the end, I did the only thing I could think to do. I took out a piece of white paper and I started to eraser. I rubbed the eraser back and forth until there was a storm of little eraser shavings, until it was little more than a nub, and then I rubbed some more. Finally, I took the paper with all the little eraser shavings over to the trash and blew. And, then, it was gone. I didn't sleep much that night, I can tell you. But, in the morning, the sun was just as bright and Poli-Sci class was just as long. The world moved on without the eraser just as it had before I knew the eraser had existed.

And that's the part that still bothers me. One day, I found an eraser in front of my locker that could've erased the world. It couldn't erased peace or joy or war or hate. Maybe it could've erased just about anything if you were willing to give it a try. And, right now, out there, there's probably another just like it or a pencil or a notebook or a coin that could change the world with a flip. Maybe there are little bits of magic all around just waiting for us to pick them up. Who knows where they come from or what they want. But they want something. They want to be picked up. They want to be used. They want to be found.

So, the next time you see something shining in the grass or by the side of the road, the next time you find something just when you need it, just let it lie. Don't even stop. Just keep walking. Trust me, you'll be glad you did.

Chapter 31:
Those Who Stir In Their Sleep

There's nothing that attracts a child more than a hidden thing. Locked doors, closed boxes, dark woods, and caves draw their thoughts and their footsteps in a way that nothing else can. Cats and children live in a world where curiosity is a thing to be reveled in—not shut away. Shiny rocks are things to pick up and ponder and possibly put in your pocket to rattle around with shells, bits of string, and robin's feathers. There's magic in the hidden. A drain pipe might not draw a grown man's gaze, but to a child, it holds a secret world. There's magic even in the mundane if you know how to look at it just right. Wardrobes and sinkholes can leads to other worlds. The wood behind your house can give way from the known to the unknown with the blink of an eye or the falling of dusk. And, there's no greater magic than in finding a stone with a hole through the center or a penny with your own birth date. There's as much magic in an old penny nail as in a magician's trick. Ask any child. There's magic everywhere.

When I was a child, there was a cave that held a particular fascination for us. It was cut into the creek bed, a tumbled down mess of limestone and scree with an opening that was easy enough for a small dog to pass through, but a good-sized girl had to wiggle to enter. Once you were inside, the tunnel opened up a bit and you could crawl and then stand. You couldn't go far though, unless you were a small dog with spirit, and even then, you were most likely called back with many a whistle and a clapping of hands. Where the cave led, we never really knew, but the air was cold as night and dark as soot. You could feel the air pressing on you and, even though the cave wasn't every deep, it felt hungry, like it wanted to swallow you up. It was, at times, enough to make even a very brave little dog shiver. But, it still drew us on and we'd dare each other to crawl inside and time who could stand it the longest.

The cave had other entrances that I didn't know about as a child. Adults fear, and rightfully so, that letting children know there are caves about is a dangerous thing. The cave itself ran under the creek and road and deep under the graveyard itself. It's a strange thing to think of a cave being under the family cemetery, and yet it was. It crept beneath the trees roots and the caskets and their occupants and stretched under the hayfields and pastures until it was too shallow to be navigated. A grown man with a lantern or flashlight and maybe a brave dog could walk quite far if he didn't fear the shadow of the dead. The dead, are mostly, silent on such things and make little account of such trespasses. Mostly.

The road that runs over the cave has had many names over the years. It's been named for weeping oaks and briars, long dead settlers, and holy men, but most folks simply calling Wagon Road. There probably hasn't been a wagon on it in more than sixty years. But it's Wagon Road just the same. Why one name stuck over the others is hard to say, but it could have something to do with the fellow who haunts it. He's been called the Riding Man for longer than anyone can remember. No one knows his name and, I suppose, he would have to be called something. I've been told that he took to riding wagons, but, now that there are no wagons left to be ridden, he'll settle for a truck, a car, or even a tractor if it's the right time of night and the moon is good and high. He never causes any trouble. He simply has a tendency to hop or fall, as some would have it, onto or into your vehicle. He'll sit politely enough until you pass the graveyard and then hop right back off. The fact that he doesn't have a head, at least not one attached to the rest of him, is troubling. But maybe it's ameliorated by the fact that he's said to always tip the hat of the head he's carrying in his arms as a sort of farewell. It's good to know that good manners can survive into the afterlife and some folks, at least, still take time to be courteous.

If you should ever find yourself driving on Wagon Road or Briar Road or Weeping Oak Road or another dark, hilly country road on a moonlight night and you should feel a slight jostle of your backseat or truck bed, there's no reason to be alarmed. You might want to give the Wagon Man a little nod to let him know you don't mind him riding along. He's sure to appreciate it. You know the old saying: You should never speak ill of the dead. After all, you don't want them speaking ill of you.

Chapter 32:
Shine A Light

Railroads have been the salvation and the doom of the South. Once the steel veins that stirred the heart of Dixie, many lay spent, rusted, and fallen to disuse. They're a cautionary tale that mirrors the South's own history—an industry that failed to keep pace with the world around it and became relegated to a means shuttling things from here to there.

It was a hard fall. Once the rail carried more than goods, it carried men and women and hopes and dreams. The rail was romance and magic. It was adventure. Riding the rail as an engineer, a porter, or even a steam house boy had a certain mystique. You were magicians able to whisk men and women cross-country in a matter of days, to carry folks literally from sea to sea.

There are a thousand ghost stories about railroads. The rails seem to carry stories as easily as they do engines and their cars. There's hardly a rail line without a legendary ghost or two or twenty, and even the smaller lines have tales to tell. Chapel Hill is just a bump in the road. There's nothing much to say about it. It's not rightly a town and surely not a city. It's just a stop on a long road with some railroad tracks and a story. Folks come from miles around to see the Chapel Hill Lights. And there are as many stories as there are folks who have claimed to have seen them.

To some, they've lit like foxfire sparking along the rails and off branches and fence rails. Others have seen strange lights in the sky hovering low and moving with strange rhythms. Some claim to have seen a bobbing light, the shape of a lantern, along the rails, and still others have seen a shape of a man, or perhaps a woman, misty and ringed with fire. What they are no one really knows. There's a story about an engineer out checking the tracks with his lantern who was hit by another train and still walks the tracks to warning people about the dangers that lurk in the night. There are other stories about aliens and sprites. Some even say the lights are the spirits of the first people who lived in the county still protesting the tracks being laid down.

Maybe one of the stories is true or maybe none of them. Or perhaps maybe the lights are the ghost of the railway itself—a sort of dry charge of all those past trips up and down the rail. Trains still use the Chapel Hill line although these days they carry auto parts, girders, and livestock instead of passengers. Maybe the rail is pining for its glory days and shining a light on what came before. One thing is for sure, if you drive up to Chapel Hill on a misty night with a full moon shining and listen, you can hear a whistling in the air. And if you're there on the right night, you may see the lights dance just for you.

Chapter 33: Shadows

There are many kinds of ghosts—ghosts of lost souls, ghosts of the land, and even the ghosts of memories. Who's to say what is or isn't a ghost? One day my sister was combing her hair when she saw a girl in rolled up jeans and Keds running a comb through her light brown hair in the mirror behind her. She was smiling and chewing gum and when she saw my sister looking at her, she blew a bubble and disappeared. My sister didn't know who she was until she saw a photo of my mom, who is very much alive, from thirty years ago. So, what was that girl? Was she a bubble in time caught as lightly as air in a piece of bubble gum? Maybe she was a memory trapped in the glass activated by another girl, close to her own age, combing her hair and chewing gum. Or maybe she was a little window into actual time and thirty years ago that girl caught a glimpse of another girl combing her hair?

Ghosts are like that. You never know what exactly you're seeing. They can appear like wisps on the wind or as solid as the person standing next to you. Many people say they don't believe in ghosts because they haven't seen one. But how do they know? The fellow sitting next to you on the bus rattling his paper could be the spirit trapped riding the rail or the echo of a passenger from last week. In the end, each of us lives in our own little box of reality. None of us knows just what anyone else sees, hears, or smells. I've been fighting with my mother for years over a certain shade of blue that she swears is green. It looks blue enough to me—as blue as the sky or a robin's egg. To her, it's a shade of green as deep as old ivy.

The first ghost I ever saw with certainly was in Leiper's Fork. I have been acquainted with the idea of ghosts since childhood. My Grandma lives next door to the family cemetery and relatives on occasion would pay her visits. We saw strange lights hovering in the laundry room, fans turn themselves on and off (sometimes when they weren't even plugged in), footsteps on the staircase and in the attic, and doors open and close. Her visitors were always the most polite of house guests, always opening and closing doors quietly and never turning over so much as a tea cup. It seemed that the kindling in her wood box was a little too full at times, too. Maybe her guests thought to add a few sticks to the pile during their visits. But I never saw any spirits. My Grandma commented on them on many occasions. She was a woman who saw ghosts. I never saw them and never cared to. Mysterious electronics were more than enough excitement for me.

There are many stories about Leiper's Fork. Folks have seen lights there, heard mysterious carriages and horses clip-clopping down the street, and seen faded images of men and women strolling passed the closed stores and dark houses chatting quietly to one another. Although Franklin and Nashville can boast a battle or two, nothing remarkable has happened in Hillsboro, as many residents of the small town still call it. It was a sleepy little place until a few years ago with a famous chef put it on the map by renovating Green's Grocery and then opening a restaurant there that received rave reviews in magazines. There were pages filled with ads for bespoke leather goods, julep cups crafted by the artisans who make the Derby cups each year, and escapes to places that balance hunting excursions with visits to the spa. A thriving antiques trade, some artisans offering custom woodwork and leather, a rare and hard-to-find book store, and a smattering of live music venues turned a few houses, a church, and a couple of meat-and-threes into a tourist destination.

But the spirits who walk the road by lamplight already knew Leiper's Fork was the place to be. They've walked the roads and old orchard for more than a hundred years. Who knows but they'll walk the same route for a hundred more?

Like Franklin, the area around Leiper's Fork was already home to settlers and entrepreneurs in the 1700s. By the 1800s, it was a thriving stop along the road to Franklin, Nashville, and Columbia—not far off from a resort offering sulphur spring treatments.

The Gray House, like many of the other houses in Leiper's Fork, doesn't look haunted. It has a gingerbread feel with a welcoming porch and a sloping front yard. A friend of mine who lived there as a girl told me stories of strange footsteps, doors and opened and shut, and whispered conversations that stopped when you came too near. The ghosts who come to visit aren't menacing. They simply are. They move things around in the kitchen, pull books from the shelves, and close windows left open after dark.

While spending the night with my friend, I saw a broom leaning against the wall stand upright by itself, tap the wall three times, and then smack back against the wall. In the fashion of any fourteen-year-old girl confronted with the supernatural, I stared hard at the broom for about an hour and then fell asleep.

Later that night, I thought I heard someone laughing on the porch. When I looked out the window, I saw a girl holding a broom and leaning against the railing. She was talking to someone under the shadowed eave of the house and laughing. She looked up and when she saw me she waved and then disappeared quick as a soap bubble. I thought I'd dreamed the entire thing until we found the broom lying on the porch in the morning.

A cousin of mine swears she saw a ghostly face peering into the window while she was at the local high school during a fall carnival. She was running a booth offering three shots at a flame with a water gun. The pale girl pressed both hands against the window, then her nose, and then disappeared in the blink of an eye. Maybe she decided she'd rather have a closer look at the carnival, or that there were better booths to spy on that the one my cousin was manning.

Every small town has its share of tragedy, but it seems that Leiper's Fork has had, on the whole, less than most. But ghosts still walk its streets, peer into the high school's windows and visit houses there. You have to wonder why. Perhaps it is because it is such a nice little town. Maybe the ghosts, like many of the people who have come to call it home, simply don't want to leave. Maybe they stroll the streets and peer in the store windows like tourists from out of town commenting on new items and even taking a quick peek inside of some of the more interesting looking stores. Maybe ladies in Victorian dresses pick up antique Limogue plates and tea cups that would've been in fashion in their day and remark on the light display each Christmas. After all, it can be hard to find a place to truly call home in this world. Maybe when you find one, you don't let a little thing like death change your address.

Chapter 34:
Unforgiven

The true mark of a Southerner is the ability to make something out of nothing. A Southern cook can take crackers, sugar, butter and need and end up with a pie that will dazzle the neighborhood. My father once made his own bellows out of an old grill and some spare bits from his tool shed. And, of course, any Southerner worth his salt can take the whisper of a slight and hold it as a grudge for the rest of his life. If he does it right, he might hold it even longer.

It was the chair, in the end, that caused the whole mess. Some say it was the dog's fault. But you can hardly blame a hound for being a hound. The chair, on the other hand, failed in every respect. It had never been a comfortable chair—razor-backed, prone to giving off splinters, and with a horsehair seat that was both slippery and scratching by turns. There are some that stand by horsehair citing its durability and luster, but I've always found the stuff hateful. And, the woman who had seated this particular chair was a weaver. She wove horsehair and wool and the hair of the dead. There was a time that it was considered a fine thing to have a pin a necklace or even a wreath made from the hair of the beloved deceased. She kept the hair and yarn all in little baskets and boxes, making the pins and necklaces by special order and presenting them set in jet and stones to grief-struck mothers and sisters and aunts. The horsehair and yarn she kept in skeins in a high shelf against the wall. But, as in any workshop, things became mingled from time to time and it was likely more than a few of her black cat's hairs ended up in horsehair seatings and more than a few hairs from the dead as well. Still, as unlucky as that may've been, it probably was the chair maker's fault for crafting such an unsteady piece of furniture. Or maybe it was the fault of the fellow who laid the stone floor which slanted north ever so slightly or the boy who salted the ham and left half a side uncovered in the brine bin. Or maybe it was just bad luck.

As it was, the very morning of "the incident," as it became later to be called, Nearest Everett got in a shouting match with his daughter's intended, a fellow named Bartok Early, which was ironic since he'd never been on time a day in his life. Early was a bright fellow but lazy as the day is long. His Granddaddy was a savvy fellow as much known for his temper as his business sense who ran a horse and mule auction, as well as a thriving bootleg business. Early was set to inherit both since his father had died young and no doubt would run both into the ground before the old man was cold in his grave. Nearest owned the only sawmill in the county. So, seemingly, it was a good match. Both the bride-to-be and her intended were well-set, and everyone said they made a handsome couple. Nearest's daughter, Elmira was known for her clever stitchwork and her auburn curls. Early was known for his sharp wit and refusal to use it for anything more than getting out of an honest day's work.

Early had a dog named Foxtrot that was as quick-witted and trouble-prone as himself. He sucked eggs, ran at cats and strangers, and nipped at horses' legs earning himself more than one kick for his pains. And if there was food of any sort to be found, Foxtrot would find it. There was never a smokehouse or chicken coop so sealed that Foxtrot couldn't gain entry. It was the thrill of the thing more than anything else that motivated him. A locked door or a sturdy gate lit a devilish delight in the dog that was matched only by his master's tolerance for his shenanigans.

The day it happened was a fine Tuesday in March. It was one of those spring days that makes a fellow glad to be alive. The sky was periwinkle blue and the clouds were high and white. It had rained a few days earlier and there was a smell of fresh grass and clean dirt in the air. It was just the kind of day that led to a fine night and Nearest meant to spend it in front of the fire drinking a fine bourbon and enjoying a smoked ham he'd been curing with brine and honey through the winter. He'd sent the boy who worked on the farm out to check on the ham that morning and give it one last good coating, and had him store the jug of bourbon he'd picked up that morning in the smokehouse. But when Nearest went to check on the ham and retrieve his jug of bourbon that night, he found the floor scattered with brine and reeking of bourbon, but of the ham and the jug there was no trace.

There had been a thief at work and Nearest immediately suspected Early. The boy was prone to jokes that few found funny, and taking a hardworking man's bourbon and ham would be exactly the sport Early would get up to. Nearest had fought with Early just that morning, saying that the boy was a ne'r-do-well and not worth his salt. Given Early's delight in irony, leaving a trail of brine might just be his way of saying he was worth his salt and a salted ham to boot. Regardless of what he had or hadn't intended, Nearest was not amused. He immediately sent the boy out to find Early and to demand he return the goods he'd stolen.

The boy found Early dawdling down by the creek with a line in the water and his hand wrapped around a cold drink, and he delivered the message. Early told the boy he didn't know anything about the bourbon or the ham—something the boy was well aware of—and demanded he tell Nearest that he had more wind than sense. The boy begged Early to come back with him and to explain that it must be an accident of some sort, but Early refused. He threw down his pole, whistled for his dog, and was off into the woods before the boy could say another word. Now, the boy was well aware of the situation and noted that Foxtrot was moving a little slower than usual, probably weighed down by the burden of half a salted ham. If he smelled a bit like a brewery, Early didn't notice. He'd been drinking a bit himself and the dog had been in the creek.

The boy knew the truth, though; he'd found the dog laying across the ham and digging in with a relish earlier that day. When he tried to shoo him off when a broom, Foxtrot had lunged at him, then grabbed the ham and backed into the corner, jostling the horsehair chair and knocking over the jug of bourbon. The boy and the dog's tug-of-war had lasted near ten minutes and had resulted in Foxtrot running off with a good sized piece of ham.

It was only after the boy inspected the ham that he noticed the bourbon jug lying half empty on its side. Given the choice of telling Nearest that he'd let a dog get in the smokehouse, eat his ham, and spill his bourbon, he chose to throw the jug and the ham down the old well and play the innocent. It was hard times everywhere and with luck, Nearest would assume a tramp had taken off with his bounty. The boy never thought that Early would be blamed. But, seeing as it was either him or Early, he decided Early was the best to bear the old man's wrath. He was, after all, only a hired boy and in need of his position. Nearest paid him in room and board, but he was learning the mule trade and it was more than he could hope. His father had lived as an indentured farmer all his life and farms were getting hard to come by—even those with clay soil and scrub brush. A boy had to look to his future.

To a man like Nearest, the loss of a ham and a jug of bourbon was no great thing. By the standards of the county, he was a prosperous fellow—but he was also proud. And the thought of Early making mischief at his expense galled him as did the young fellow's smug face and his all-too-ready smile. It seemed to Nearest that Early had too many square white teeth and he was all too fond of showing them. His easy laugh, which had captured Nearest's daughter's heart, reminded the old farmer of the braying of a jackass. He thought, at first, to let the slight go, but after seeing Nearest leaning against his fence mid-day without a thought to put in an honest day's work anywhere, he decided that he needed to teach him a lesson.

184

Nearest had a hired man named Merritt who was reckoned a fine shot. He'd been lauded in turkey shoots across the county and many fellows spoke of his skill with firearms, as well as with powder and bow. The fellow was also known to have tastes that outstripped his pocket. He liked to gamble, drink fine bourbon, and court ladies who demanded gifts of quality. Nearest, with an eye at teaching Early a lesson, promised this man three jugs of the finest Kentucky bourbon if he'd give Early a good scare. Early was known to play cards at a certain house of questionable trade twice a week, and to walk home with no company other than his good-for-nothing hound, Foxtrot. Nearest convinced this fellow to lay in wait for Early and to fire a shot or two at him—maybe breaking a jug he might be carrying or, if it was possible, knocking his cap askew. It would be fine recompense, Nearest thought, for the grief the young fellow had caused him and a good lesson not to lay up carousing half the night.

The problem was that it was a cold night. Merritt had been given one jug as an incentive with the other two to be paid after Nearest heard the story from Early's own mouth the next day. But a fellow laying in wait on a cold spring night might be inclined to take a sip or two or three of a comforting jug by his side and without realizing it, not be as steady on the draw as he would have been an hour or two earlier. And, as luck would have it, Early was late leaving the game that night. It was near morning when he and Foxtrot started home and the full moon had started to set. Merritt was half a jug down and half asleep when Foxtrot caught his scent and let out the deep howl that hounds use when they pick up the smell of danger. Foxtrot smelled metal and gunpowder and whiskey, and even a hound knows that's no good combination.

The dog took off running toward the copse of pines where Merritt was waiting and so fierce was his charge that Merritt fired off a shot above the dog's head to warn him off. Unfortunately, with his eyes bleary from sleep and drink he failed to see Early on the heels of the big red coon hound until the bullet had already left his gun. It seemed to Merritt later that the smoke from the gun hung on the air like an accusation, that he could see the hound lunging slowing toward him, and that he almost felt Early's last breathe graze his cheek. When the boy fell to the ground, the hound turned and ran back to his master and let out a sound so mournful that Merritt reckoned its echo burrowed into the very bones of the earth. Merritt took off running with the cries of the hound following on his heels.

The next day, folks found Early in the grass, dead from a single shot with the great red hound crouched over him. The dog was so fearsome that no man dared approach and it was finally Early's betrothed, Nearest's own daughter, who put a rope around the dog's neck and led him away so that Early's body could be brought home. He was buried on a Thursday and during the closing of the grave Foxtrot let out a low howl that shook the very woods and then went silent. The next three days the sky opened up and delivered a torrent of biblical proportions so that Nearest, his daughter, and Foxtrot dared not leave the house even to fetch firewood. The rain pelted the house and the creek swoll to the size of a proper river. Footlogs were washed from one side of the county to the next and Nearest's smokehouse was dragged clean away by the angry river. Foxtrot lay sullen by the fire casting suspicious glances Nearest's way. If his daughter noticed, she said nothing. She only sat crying and petting the red hound.

Years went by and the hound never failed to visit his master's grave. As soon as Nearest's daughter, Elmira opened the door, Foxtrot would make his way up the gravel road to the family cemetery and keep vigil until dusk. He'd return home tired and hungry and ready to stare at Nearest with eyes that knew the truth. Although Merritt had left the county that very night, it was Nearest who heard the dog howling and picked up the whiskey jug. He hadn't wanted the boy dead, it was true, but he didn't mourn him either. Still, every time he felt the dog's brown eyes on him, Nearest's throat went dry and his eyes burned. He begged his daughter to give the dog to Early's brother for her own peace of mind, but the girl wouldn't hear of it. She doted on the red hound from the day Early died until Foxtrot met his end some ten years later. He died a dog more gray than red with tired feet from climbing the gravel road each day to sit by his master's side. Even after his death, folks swore for years that when the sun shone on Early's grave, you could see the shadow of a large dog with his head resting on his paws. And for the rest of Nearest's life he heard the patter of the dog's long nails on the wood floorboards of his house, and felt the dog's bitter stare on the back of his neck. His daughter eventually married and left him, but the spirit of the dog never did, and on his death bed, it was to Early and Foxtrot that Nearest called out, not to his mother or wife or even his daughter who had died in childbirth years before.

After Nearest died, the story surrounding Bartok Early's grave changed a bit. Folks still said that you could see a dog's shadow if the sun or the moon was shining high, but that you could see a man beside the hound with his hand resting on its head and every now and again, if you watched closely enough, you could see the dog's tail wag.

Chapter 35:
Wake the Dead

Prosper Vance was not a young man. But he wasn't an old one either. He'd sat as sheriff for the county for forty long years coming straight off of a hitch with the Army. He'd put down one gun and taken up another and a cause along with it, though he didn't suppose he'd known that at the time. He'd sworn with his hand on a Bible to protect and serve, and, he reckoned he'd done his best. He hadn't realized all those years ago just what service really entailed. That he had given up a piece of his life and maybe a bit of his soul to the folks in the county. That boy of forty years ago may've understood he was signing on for long days and sleepless nights, but there was no way he could've fathomed how dark men's hearts could be or how the sight of a gold band laying on your palm could fill you with a cold despair for which there were no words.

Prosper thought about that boy sometimes and he wondered if he would've made the long drive to Old Man Everett's place or if he would've dared to ask for so dark a favor. Prosper was not a church-going man, but he believed in God all the same. He'd sat with his Mama and brothers through a childhood of tent revivals and Sunday sermons. He knew for a fact that Heaven and Hell were as real as the lines on his face though he often thought they existed as much in the here and now as in the hereafter. He couldn't imagine there were devils any worse than the black-hearted men who walked among us or angels kinder than folks he'd seen forgive time and time again those that did them wrongs so great that Prosper had to steel his own heart not to take a vengeance for them.

A sheriff's badge was a heavy thing. It bound the man to the law whether that law was just or not. Prosper reckoned that there were some who just didn't deserve to walk this green earth. But that was not his decision to make. He'd taken up his burden and bound it to his chest. And, after forty years, they were as wed as any for better or for worse.

There was no reason, really, to have doubted the facts of this case. They were hard and cold and clean. Amy Green was dead. Plain and simple. There was no need to call it murder, and yet murder, Prosper believed, it was. It pricked at him. That was it in the end. He had no proof and no reason to doubt the coroner's words or his own eyes, but there it was. Even after the case was closed and Amy safely put to rest, Prosper could not let it be. He read his case notes each night and he found that any walk he started would take him past Amy Green's house with its white-washed fence and little tire swing. He saw her widowed husband walking their puppy, a dog Prosper had seen the girl playing with on the town green not a month before, and it caught at the edges of his mind. In the end, the only reasoning he had was the simplest arithmetic—it just didn't add up. A happy girl, just married, with the sold sign still on her new lawn and a bright pup in the yard does not walk out into Silver Pond and drown. She just doesn't.

Amy Green had a common, happy life. It was not the stuff of stories. It was the welt and waft of reality. She worked at the bank, she walked her dog, she shopped at the local Piggly Wiggly on Thursdays, and she was happy. She was happy. Any fool could see it. But one night she had laid her wedding ring on the kitchen table, locked the doors behind her, and walked barefooted down the long gravel drive and then down the Interstate Road. She'd climbed the split rail fence surrounding the Hayborne pasture and walked straight into the pond. She kept walking until she was at the center where her feet couldn't touch the ground and then she'd let go sinking into the goose grass and mud. If she had any final words, only the frogs and catfish heard them.

Her husband found her ring on the kitchen table, the car in the drive, and Amy gone the next day and raised the alarm.

Even though only a few hours had passed, Prosper and his deputies started their search. Amy was not the kind of girl to leave in a huff. She was a careful woman, a bank teller and a regular member of the Clearmont Primitive Baptist. She volunteered at the community center once a month when local relief passed out necessities to those who needed them, carefully sorting out bags of flour and rice, boxes of cheese, and cans of beans and putting them in cardboard boxes for the folks who would come by throughout the day.

It was Prosper's newest deputy, Michael Allen who found her floating in the pond, her long black hair tangling with the weeds. When Prosper arrived at the scene, the boy was weeping, but, as he'd been taught, he'd left the body as it was found, though you could tell it pained him. The coroner confirmed what Prosper's own eyes could see—there wasn't a mark on her other than her bloodied feet. She had simply walked into the water and let go. She left no note, only the ring and a fresh bowl of food and water for the pup. There was simply no call for it, and, after forty years of suicides, homicides, robberies, and lies, Prosper knew the smell of a case that just didn't add up.

He didn't mean to take the ring. It should've been given back to Amy's husband or slipped on her hand in the casket. But the bereaved man didn't think of the ring and it had remained tagged and sealed in an evidence bag along with the clothes Amy had been wearing and the barrettes from her hair. Prosper had found the ring along with the other things when he was closing out the case, slipped it from its bag, and after a moment of thought, dropped it into his pocket. He could not have imagined the heaviness of that small band of gold. He felt it whispering to him on his long drive, but he didn't turn back. He couldn't now. They say the dead don't talk, but Prosper knew that wasn't rightly true. They speak to us every day. A piece of ribbon, a quilt of calico and velvet, or a tin soldier can hold the weight of a thousand conversations past and others

190

never completed. But it wasn't memory and regret that drove Prosper on. It was certainty.

Prosper had seen things in his life that he could not explain. He didn't let them worry him much. Life was filled with mysteries, and God had not made men to understand them all. Still, he knew of a man who understood more than most. He was what country folk called uncanny, and what Prosper called a witch. There was a time that Prosper hadn't believed all the talk about Old Man Everett, but that day was long past. He'd seen with his own eyes what the man could do. Here was a man who could wake the dead and put them to rest. Whether it was right or wrong Prosper didn't know. It was probably best for men not to meddle in such things, but here he was with a cold ring in his pocket and a mind full of doubt. And ahead he could see Old Man Everett's cabin and he knew somehow that the old man would be waiting for him.

The old man was sitting still as a statue in his rocker. If the moon hadn't been high, Prosper mightn't have seen him. He was a shadow in the darkness with only the lit end of his cigarette to betray him when he took a long drag. Prosper shut the truck door and the sound seemed to linger on the night air. It took him a long time to walk to that porch, and all that time the old man said nothing. But when Prosper reached the steps, he stood and ground out his cigarette.

Prosper stood staring at the old man for a long time and then said, "I reckon you know why I'm here."

"Reckon I do," he said. "I conjure you think you did me a favor."

"I never did you any favors," Prosper said. "That I do know."

"I guess not," the old man replied. "But all the same, here you are with that girl's ring in your hand."

Prosper stared at him. "You don't miss much."

"I don't miss anything." The old man shook his head slowly. "Leastwise, nothing that happens in this Valley. I make it a point not to."

Prosper held out the ring, a simple band of white gold, and the old man took it and held it up under the light. "A thing of blood and bone," the old man said, "That's what this is. You want me to call that poor girl from her rest for this. For a truth you already know."

"I don't know; that's why I'm here." He added, "If I knew, if there was some way to know, then some son-of-a-bitch would be in the jail."

"You know," the old man said somberly. "And that's why you're here. If you didn't know what this was, then you would'na drove up here in the dark with the weight of a dead girl hanging around you like a storm."

"All right then," Prosper said, "I do know what it is— murder, plain and simple. But I can't prove it. The coroner and the law have ruled it natural causes, but you and I both know there's nothing natural about it."

"That is so."

"So, you'll do what you can?" Prosper asked.

The old man hesitated, and then nodded. "I will for the girl, and for you, and because there's a law for these things as well. Though like all laws, it can be broke." The old man reached for another cigarette and Prosper could see his hand was steady as a stone. "I could tell you what you need to know," the old man said, "but I reckon you need to hear it from her own lips. You didn't drive all this way in the dark to talk to me."

Prosper nodded, and the old man held out the ring to him. "There's some that might need such a thing, but I'm not one of them," he said flatly. "The dead come when I call. whether they like it or not." Prosper took the ring and sat down on the stair while the old man lit another cigarette. Everett took a drag and said, "Filthy habit. I quit near on thirty years ago, before my boy was born, but I found I had a need for the things again. You can quit and start many a thing if you live long enough. Life's a long path, and a winding one."

The old man picked up a twisted ash cane that was leaning against the railing and set to drawing a circle in the dirt, every now and again stopping to flick ash into the red soil. After a few minutes he stood back, took a look at the circle and then crushed out the rest of his cigarette on edge of the thing. He stepped into the circle and then said some words that Prosper later couldn't remember, although when he thought back on the moment it seemed like he'd felt the words more than heard them. They were great, slow things that cut through the air like water through stone. There was a crack like lightning striking a tree and then Prosper could see a figure coming reluctantly up the dirt path like it was being pulled by wire. The shadow twisted and pulled but kept coming forward while the old man stood impassive in the circle looking down the road. After awhile he moved his hand and the figure sped up, as if he was a fisherman reeling in his catch.

Finally, the girl stood before them on the outer edge of the circle looking as she had the day they pulled her out of the Pond. Shoeless, dressed in a dark skirt and a pale blouse, she stood wringing her hands and looking back toward the way she'd come. "We'll let you go soon enough," the old man said, "Only this fellow has a few questions to ask you. I reckon you know what they're about, as you know who he is. There's no getting away from the law." The old man added, "Not even in the grave."

The girl scrunched her face like she was about to cry, but said nothing. After a while she nodded and the old man said, "Ask your questions then."

Prosper stood and started down the stairs toward the girl. He knelt in the dirt in front of her with his hand in his pocket wrapped around the ring. Finally, he held it out to her. "I never meant to take it," he said. The girl reached out and plucked the ring off his outstretched palm. The moment she touched him, Prosper felt a light shock and smelled lilies and fresh spring dirt. The girl smiled and put the ring on her finger. "You left it on the table," Prosper said. After she had nodded and held her ring hand up to the light, admiring it, he asked, "Why?"

The girl who had been Amy Green wrapped her arms around herself and shivered though the air was warm. "I never meant to leave it," she said, "I never meant to go. But it was always in my mind, every moment of the day. I could feel it even in my sleep and, in the end, there was no other way to get away. I never asked for it. I never wanted it. I prayed and prayed and prayed, but it just wouldn't stop and in the end it was the only thing I could think to do."

"What wouldn't stop?" Prosper asked.

The girl looked sad and glanced away. "He's not a bad man," she said, "I can see that now. But I didn't love him. I told him I never would, but he just kept at me. At first there were notes and flowers and later I could hear him whispering in my head, '*Love me, love me, love me.* But I didn't. I would've if I could just to stop the whispers. But it just wasn't in me. I thought he would give up after the wedding, but he didn't. He just kept whispering until it was all I could hear. It was the worst at night. But it was there all the time. All the time." She shivered.

"Who?" Prosper asked and she gave him the name he'd already know in his heart.

The old man moved his hand, but the girl didn't move. When she whispered, "You should have saved me," Prosper blanched until he saw she was looking at the old man.

"I could have," he said, "But I didn't. There's no malice in it. I was occupied with other things. Mostly with feeling sorry for myself. I let things slip that I shouldn't have and you were caught between them."

The girl nodded and started down the path and Prosper watched her until she was gone. Behind him, the old man said, "I won't make any excuses. A man has to bear his burdens."

"I can't understand it," Prosper said.

The old man just shook his head and sighed. "Don't see why not. You're a smart fellow and a witch is easy to understand. There's one thing all witches have in common— they're folks that just can't let well enough be. They kick against the pricks instead of just letting them slide. They're meddlesome. Could be some think they're meddling for good. Others have a mind only for themselves or maybe they don't think much about it at all. But at the core of it is a great want, a great emptiness that they can't quite fill. Lots of men have it. Some turn to drink, some turn to religion, and others turn to witching. Once you start down that path, there's no end to it. There's just the need and that little whispering voice in the dark that says "Just one more." But it's never just one more drink or prayer or spell. In the end, the only way any man can stand is on his own two feet. The rest is just cowardice."

Prosper didn't say anything for a long time and then just as he was about to speak, he decided better of it. "That's right," the old man said, "I should know. But knowing doesn't make you stop. Maybe it only makes you more arrogant. I've been where this fellow is. I've walked in his shoes, and he's not going to stop, not anytime soon anyway."

"You're not a bad man, Everett," Prosper said.

The old man said nothing. He turned his back and walked a little down the path and then he stopped. "You see that moon?" he asked. It was hard not to see. It hung full and low and orange-red in the sky. "That's a harvest moon," he said. "There's a harvest moon and a wolf moon and a cold moon each year, but not like this. This is a true harvest moon full of bitterness and blood. Because, it's been my experience, that's the only real harvest there is in the end. The path may be long and it has many a turn, but in the end, we all end up in the same place." He turned his back on Prosper and twisted his walking stick in the dirt. "I'm tired."

Prosper knew that he was an old man, though no one in the Valley knew just how old. Even the grannies who sold herbs and dumplings in the market on fair day called him the old man. Some claimed that he was older than the valley itself. But men are prone to telling tales around a wood stove with a bottle of whiskey passed hand to hand. No one lived forever.

"That's right," the old man said as if he'd heard Prosper thinking. "There's not a fellow save Elijah who never died, though there are words to wake the dead. This is an old magic called up out of the dark places of the earth. It has no name and the words are as old as the flickering of flames, the churning of waters, and the fiercest of storms. They are built into the fabric of things. Men were never meant to hear them, let alone utter them. They are the words of God. But men are curious creatures prone to meddle where they shouldn't. Some say that fire was God's gift to man, others that man found it, and others that it was stolen. But of these words there can be no debating. They were given. Spoken to raise a man. Once heard, they can never be forgotten. They burn and whisper in dreams. They're hungry words. The only way to be free of them is to give them to someone else and until you do, you'll never die."

The old man stopped a bit and stared up at the moon. Prosper stood as still as an oak, uttering not a sigh. He had a feeling the old man had never told this story before, not even to his son, maybe especially not to his son. There was a weight to his tale that bore on the air and made Prosper feel, for a moment, as ancient as the stones and as weary as the old man himself. The old man turned his back to Prosper again, and stood looking at the moon for a long time. He finally spoke, "Most men think that immortality is a wonderful thing. But men weren't built for it. It's hard enough to live and love and hate all in a span of three score and ten or twenty or thirty. After that, a man starts to go ragged around the edges like a piece of cloth too long in use. He starts to think that those words that he begged and bargained for weren't a gift. Maybe they were a curse. He starts to remember the way the fellow he had them off of smiled and sighed when he whispered them in his ear, and that when he crumbled slowly into the red dust the look on his face hadn't been one of despair, but one of desperate relief."

Prosper said nothing, only waited. After a while the Old Man continued, "Of course a man of twenty or even twenty and ten doesn't notice things like that. But they stick in the mind's eye and creep up on you years later so that the last thing you see when close your eyes is the look on that old man's face—a look so full of hope and peace that you long for it. You look for it in the mirror each and every day, but all you see is tired eyes and a bitter scowl because you know deep down in your bones what it means to pass the words along. You know what a horror it is to live through the ages, but you just can't bring yourself to do it. Not because you're afraid, but because you're afraid of being that cruel to another living soul."

The old man turned back to him. "You may think you know a thing about cruelty, Sheriff. But you surely don't. A good man may think he can understand such a thing, but he never can."

"All men sin," Prosper said.

"They do," said the old man, "But only one with a good soul would admit it." He waited a minute or maybe ten and then he said, "We best be going while the moon's high. Tonight is a night of power, for him and me. If it's to be done, then we best get to it. He'll be waiting by now."

"Why would he?" Prosper asked.

The old man looked back and his smile chilled Prosper to the bone, "Because," he said, "He knows just as plain as you and me that there's only one way for this story to end."

The old man walked and Prosper followed. The air was heavy and damp like it gets sometimes in early October right before a storm. Prosper could hear the old man breathing heavy and sometimes he leaned hard on his cane, but in the end, they came to the graveyard, as he knew they would, and he could see a man standing with his hand on Amy Green's grave. Even from this distance, Prosper could hear him weeping big ragged sobs and every now and again he'd strike the rough-cut granite with his fist.

"I didn't mean it," he said.

"Doesn't matter," Prosper told him, "What you meant and what you done are two separate things. She's dead all the same and none's to bring her back."

The boy looked at the old man with hope, "You could," he said, "I know you could."

The old man shook his head, "I conjure I could," he said, "But I've tried that before and it never turns out the way you'd hope. Might be this time that she'd come back the same sweet soul she always was, but maybe she wouldn't. Like as not, she wouldn't thank you for it. She's at rest now. Let her go."

The boy knelt and wept, and after a time he pushed himself up. He wiped his eyes with the back of his fist. It left a smear of mud beside one eye. "I only meant to make her love me," he said. "It's all I wanted. Just for her to love me like I love her."

"You can't push a thing against its nature, son," the old man said, "Sometimes you can bend it for awhile, but sooner or later it will snap clean in two."

The boy nodded and started to weep again. "What will happen now?" he whispered. To Prosper he looked pitifully young, and, he supposed he was. But young or not, he still had a death on his hands, and sorry or not, he had to account for it.

The old man looked at him hard. "You knew what you were doing when you did it and damned the consequences. You only cared for yourself and maybe you should have a taste of the same medicine, for surely there's not a court made that would believe the truth of it."

The boy kept on sobbing. Looking at him standing with his hand on the grave and the other against his chest, it was easy to forget that he had one death already to his name. One, anyway, that Prosper could lay at his feet. It would be simple to forget except for the empty space in Prosper's pocket that kept reminding him. The weight of the ring was even heavier now that it was gone.

"He's young," the old man said, "There's some that might say that given time, he might change his ways."

"And, what would you say?" Prosper asked, "What do you think would come of such a fellow with time."

"Likely, more dead folk," the old man said, "But I been wrong before. And, I've never taken it on myself to be the judge of another man."

"Maybe that's just the problem," Prosper said. "Maybe you ought to have at one time or another."

"You wouldn't be the first to say so," the old man said, "But that would make me no better than this boy and we both know that love and pride have led me down roads I knew better than to take."

Prosper said, "I been doing this a long time. Some days, most days lately, I think too long. It's not the place of the law to judge a man's right or wrong, just to gather the facts. And, I reckon, we both seen what's true tonight, though no jury ever will."

The old man nodded. "You done your work, Sheriff," he said, "and, whether you believe it or not, I do owe you a debt. The laws that govern my kind are old and when a man decides to buck them, there's a price to be paid. There has to be a balance to things and even if that black-haired girl laid down the coin this fella was owning, that doesn't make his debt paid in full. Go on home, Sherriff. I'll see things put as right as they can be."

Sometime during the conversation the boy had started listening to them and he now stood still and wide-eyed in the moonlight. Prosper almost felt some pity for him. Almost. He turned his back and then walked back down the path. After a while, a cloud passed over the moon and all was dark save the stars. It was a long walk back to the old man's cabin and a longer drive back to Prosper's own home. He didn't mind, though. He was in no mood to face sleep. He thought some day he might have to ask the old man what became of the boy, but maybe he didn't want to know. There were truths in this world too fearsome for a mortal man, and mercies too terrible. Maybe it was enough to know that his was not the only law and that the dead could forgive you. Or maybe it wasn't.

Chapter 36:
Ghosts

We live in little boxes. We hunker down and pull the covers over our heads and listen to the wind howling outside out windows, believing we're safe. But there is no security. We live on a stone hurtling through time and space with the universe screaming around us. We're tethered by the merest of strings—by gravity and faith in unseen forces as tenuous as the stirrings of the human heart. We are in the dark and afraid, but we are not alone. There are others in the night with us, for good or ill. They circle and stare, embrace us, cower, weep, and stand as a light in the endless night that is human existence. We believe that death is an ending or a beginning, but it is neither. It is the middle of a long journey that began before us and will end long after we are forgotten.

The dead lie under our feet. We breathe the dust that was once men and beasts, they become a part of us with every breath we take, and yet we claim that this moment in time has significance—and it does. They all do. Every moment, every second, and even the tiniest microns of measurable time matter. They are all we have. We are now. We have a few bright minutes to burn, to love and weep, to hate and scream, to exist. The marks we make are forever and our good or evil echoes on through eternity. If nothing matters then everything matters as well. All we can control is what we are, what we do, what we dare to believe. The imprint of that belief lives on as the ghost of laughter and tears. It takes hold on the world and walks and sighs and sings even when we are dust. We walk among the ghosts of dinosaurs and kings. If you close your eyes and listen, you can hear the echo of a thousand, thousand dead worlds and perhaps they can hear you as well. After all, who's to say who the ghosts really are?

We're all dying. From the morning we're born until our own personal end of days, we're rushing toward a finality we can't escape. Men and women, beasts and trees, even mountains die with time. We are all worn down by the inevitable march of days, but we glory in them as well. We are all, a bit, in love with death, with time, with the end of things. There's nothing more exciting than an ending. A beginning can't quite cast the same fascination as the final curtain whether it falls on applause, dismay, or utter silence. That's why ghost stories hold such a fascination—because they hold a clue to our own endings.

We all say we love a good "happily ever after," but in the end, it isn't the happy stories we return to again and again. It's the stories with bittersweet endings because all endings *are* bittersweet. This is the truth the dead know by heart. They understand that the best part of the story isn't the beginning or the ending—it's the middle, the everyday. The dead dream of quiet days and long nights and the simple pleasures of falling leaves and a child's smile. They return to houses where they folded laundry and cooked simple meals, they walk school hallways where they carried books and worried over lost term papers, they sit on park benches, and they watch us live and love and take every breath for granted. They try to warn us, but we won't listen. Instead we hustle from day to day and hour to hour hoping for the end of the work week, the semester, the year until we stand in their shoes, looking into windows where we once lived and worked and slept.

We are our own ghosts. Every day you wish away, every moment you take for granted, is a haunted one. We are the walking dead—lifeless, tired, and longing for the end of the day. Every wasted moment is another nail in our coffins. The hungry ghost at the window is your own reflection. Your breath on the glass is no proof of life. Life is for the living. It's a pity we don't seem to realize that until too late.

Not all ghosts have sad stories and bitter endings. Some simply choose not to end. A friend of mine once took me to a theatre who everyone swore was haunted by the ghost of a little boy. He only appeared to the women and girls, usually when they were cleaning up after a show. He'd hide behind between the seats and sometimes pile crushed Junior Mint and popcorn boxes near the trash cans to make their jobs a little easier. Even when they didn't see him, they could hear him laughing. Maybe he chose to return to the place he enjoyed the most to relive bright moments, like a film playing over and over through time.

A co-worker told me that the last building where he'd worked had been haunted by a past Chairman of the Board. In life, he'd been an erasable fellow prone to tapping his heavy cane on the floor when he wanted a cup of coffee or some dictation taken. When he died, his books and papers were cleared away, but each night he'd return to his office. The cleaning crew refused to touch the place and my friend swore that while he was working late one night he could hear a party going on in that office. Glasses clinked, corks were popped, and laughter rang out through the dark hallways. He didn't stay long enough to see if the spirits would issue him an invitation or not.

Somewhere a little boy is playing in a theatre and eating Junior Mints and juju beads forever. Somewhere there's a party where there's no last call and the music never stops. Those are some ghosts who know how to live.

Chapter 37:
More than Molasses

Avery held her cell phone above her head and counted slowly to ten. It was sleek model ordered in a pale pink platinum that complimented her hair, and it was at this time totally and utterly useless. No signal. No signal for at least the last thirty miles. Avery cursed, turned the phone on and off, and then cursed again. Ahead, she could see a sign proclaiming "The South's Best Cookin'—Satisfaction Guaranteed" which she severely doubted was true. She flicked her eyes up to check her navigation as a perfectly modulated voice advised her to "Turn left here."

Even with the air conditioner turned to full it was stifling, cloying. There was something about the South that always set ill with her—a full-bodied heat that pressed down on you and just wouldn't let up. And, it was more than just heat. It was...she wasn't sure what...something as creeping and insidious as kudzu that pulled you under and made you just want to give up. This must be what drowning feels like, Avery thought, and not for the first time.

She hated this assignment. She hated the South and its entire deep-fried persona. It was her own fault for pissing off her editor, for calling him a fat bastard and for hurling her one of her favorite Manolo's at him. But, then, he was sleeping with her sister and more importantly he'd called her a bleach-headed narcissist with more degrees than sense. Avery took offense at that. Her highlights had cost nearly half a paycheck.

But in the end it hadn't mattered. An assignment was an assignment, and keeping a permanent gig was more important than pride. Avery remembered her freelance days, living from story to story and paycheck to paycheck. Mike might be a jerk and a cheater, but he was a good editor and he had a proverbial nose for a story. The South was hot now, literally and figuratively, and a food reporter could ill-afford to ignore the sudden obsession the well-heeled had developed for hoe-cakes, collard greens, and barbecue. Granted, those dishes were most likely served with a side of persimmon and peach chutney or a demi-glaze of saffron and bacon-infused bourbon, but no matter how gussied up they might appear on the pages of *Garden & Gun*, they still hailed from states below the Mason-Dixon line. And as much as Avery might hate it, this was where she was from. You couldn't escape it really—your roots. Like actual roots they snarled at you and pulled you back, twinning around your ankles and hauling you miles from where you could get a cup of coffee and instead had to settle for sweet tea, chicory, or a cup of Joe—a beast so divorced from the lattes she sipped at Peet's that she doubted they had more in common than they had both been ground from some sort of bean.

She was home all right, even though it wasn't home anymore. She recognized the slightly rotten smell of magnolia and wisteria that no amount of cigarette smoke could overpower. Not that she didn't try, taking a drag off her third cigarette and flicking the ashes onto the bubbling asphalt. Car and phone equally dead, she stripped off her jacket and prepared to hail the next pick-up truck that came along. She didn't have long to wait. Before she had time to finish number three she saw a big ole Ford come belching up the road. Your typical farm truck, it had more engine than paint, a toolbox bolted on the back, and a gun rack above the seat. A tattered blue tarp was strung from the toolbox to the gate and underneath Avery could see what she hoped was a load of dirt. She held up her cell, thought better of it, and then stuck out her thumb. The truck slowed, and then pulled over. The driver, a sun-browned man somewhere between thirty and fifty wearing a grayed gimmee cap and coveralls, leaned out. "Having some trouble, missus?" he asked.

Avery held her tongue, flashed her best smile, and answered, "My car died. I was hoping you could give me a lift to the restaurant down the road. I'm sure they'd let me use their phone."

The man looked at the Droid clutched in her hand, "Not much good out here," he said. "Had one myself for a while, but it didn't have the reach I needed. Besides, I like to do my talking face to face." He smiled again and Avery saw he had a gold tooth. "Besides," he said with a laugh, "you're along the road for me, and I never mind having company on the way."

Avery smiled and nodded while he got out and opened the door. The truck was high. Too high for a woman in heels and a pencil skirt, but there was no help for it. Avery hiked her skirt, grabbed the door frame, and swung herself up. The man looked impressed. It was like a bike, really, Avery thought. You never really forgot how to mount a horse or a pick-up truck. Avery pulled the door shut and let the air conditioning wash over. She was amused to see that the gun rack held a twisted walking stick and not the usual 30/30. The driver smiled and patted the steering wheel. "Don't worry, missus," he said, "she's more reliable than my own two feet. She'll get you where you need to go every time."

"I just want to call a tow truck and my editor," Avery said.

The man nodded, "There's no better place to find story than Luli's."

"As long as there's a phone," Avery said.

"I'm sure you'll find what you're looking for," he answered, "and if I were you, I'd never turn down a glass of sweet tea on a day like this. In my experience, a person should never refuse something to eat, a bit of sleep, or a kind word. You never know when the next one will be coming your way."

"Maybe," Avery said, but before she could finish the driver waved his hand to the left.

"There she is," he said and pointed. The restaurant, if it could be called that, was not on her list. Avery doubted that it would have been on anyone's list. It was a concrete building painted a peeling pink with a hand-lettered plywood sign reading simply: OPEN. Not that you would've needed the sign, since the gravel parking lot was packed. The pick-up truck double-parked behind a bright yellow SUV with gold rims and red lettering on the side proclaiming it "Si's Ride."

"Don't worry," the driver said. "We'll be gone before the Si finishes his fried pie." He turned the ignition off and walked around to open Avery's door. "It's been a pleasure, missus," he said with a tip of his cap.

"Aren't you going in?" Avery asked.

The man shook his head. "There's places I have to be," he said with a laugh. "Tell Luli I said hello." He nodded again and swung back up into the pick-up.

"Thank you," Avery said again, but the truck was already pulling away. Avery watched it go then straightened her skirt, stowed her phone, and headed toward the door. It was a bright blue in the pink face of the restaurant and when she pulled it the cool air settled around her shoulders like a shawl. Avery sighed and stepped inside. Behind her, the door closed with a tinkling of bells. There was a sign that said, simply, "Seat yourself if you please." And, so Avery did.

She picked up a menu and looked around. The tables were a mash-up of sixties linoleum and wood paired with chairs and benches that looked like they'd be more at home at a flea market. The walls were hung with paintings in old and new frames, on blocks of wood and tin. Here and there pieces of paper were tacked up with hand-drawn images, some better than others. A few looked like a child's drawing in crayon. Avery studied them all with an eye towards writing an article. Maybe it was an attempt to be ironic, a take on the Museums of Curiosities you see springing up in the corners of the South, housing bleached animal bones, portraits on rusted saw blades, and bits of flotsam and jetsam found and made. There was no questioning the place's success though. Every seat was filled now that she'd taken the half-table against the wall. She looked down at the menu. It was hand-written and smudged with jam and coffee-stains. A pink sticker on the front proclaimed "Fresh biscuits all day long."

That's what she really wanted, she thought, a biscuit, a real biscuit made with lard and flour with just a pinch of salt. A low, slightly squared biscuit like her Granna used to make, rolling them out with a hickory pin and cutting them with a knife—not these mile-high store biscuits or the gourmet kind seasoned with curry and basil. But a real, Southern biscuit with a little blackberry jam on the side a nice pat of butter. God knows she hadn't eaten one in years. How could you even assign a point value to such a thing? Her personal trainer would die if he even knew she was considering it. But here she was with her mouth literally watering.

The waitress, and there only seemed to be one, stormed out of the kitchen, her arms piled with plates which she distributed around the room with a grace that only a veteran of a thousand lunches could've summoned. Avery had to admire her style. Trailing steam, the girl looked as though she'd just left her stylist. Her jet hair was piled high and decorated with jewel-toned clips, her nails and lipstick matched exactly and her three-inch heels sang a staccato on the hardwood floor. Avery tried hard not to stare when she stopped at her table. "Your hair is beautiful," Avery said. The girl, now free-handed, gave her curls a pat. "I did it myself," she said, "but I appreciate you saying so. You know what you want?"

Avery didn't hesitate. She ordered biscuits and unsweetened tea. But at the last minute changed it to sweet tea—damn the calories. The girl set down a glass of water and within a minute or two returned with a pitcher of tea and a plate of biscuits flecked with butter and honey. Avery ate the first biscuit so quickly she burned her tongue and the second with a slowness that was almost painful. It was more than a piece of bread. It was home in bite-sized pieces.

Home. She'd thought she didn't miss it. Lord knows she'd left as soon as she could, her diploma stowed in her Samsonite hard-side. She'd traded cotton blouses and Mary Janes for cashmere and Jimmy Choos and been glad of it—or so she thought. Why then were these biscuits bringing tears to her eyes? Outside, it started to rain. She could smell the clean, sweet smell that clay gives off when the summer rain hits it mixed with fresh-cut hay and magnolias and something that reminded her of her Granna's perfume. She looked up from her plate and saw a woman standing in front of her table, apron dusted with flour, hair pinned up with bobby pins and covered with a faded blue bandana.

"It's nice to have your work truly appreciated," she said. "Come back to my kitchen?"

Avery nodded biscuit crumbs on her chin. She stood and wiped her face with a red checkered napkin. "Forgettin' something?" the woman asked. Avery was. She reached down and picked up the biscuit basket and followed the cook.

The kitchen was empty. Pots steamed, kettles whistled, and a cauldron bubbled over an open fire with a gumbo so rich you felt like you'd gained five pounds from one whiff. Luli opened a wall oven and pulled out a cast-iron cornbread skillet and another shaped like ears of corn. She flipped the sweet bread onto a blue and white platter and set it on the counter. Soon enough Avery heard the tap, tap, tap of the waitress' heels and the bread disappeared. "It's just you back here?" Avery asked.

"Just me," Luli said. "Been just me for a long time now. But I have company enough," she said gesturing toward the crowd upfront. "Folks come here 'cause they're hungry. Maybe they don't even know what for. They have it in their mind they want one thing and then order something different. Maybe it comes to them that there's something they've been wanting for years without even knowing it. Maybe it's something they can't even admit to themselves. But I can tell you this, girl, no one leaves my place hungry. Everyone who comes here can push back from the table knowing they couldn't stand even one more bite—though maybe they'd want to."

Avery could smell an article. A local restaurant specializing in homegrown and seasonal fare with a single plucky cook and her daughter for a waitress and, dare she hope, an organic garden in the back.

"She's not my daughter," Luli said. "Just a girl for the front."

"What?" Avery asked. "I, oh, I didn't mean to make assumptions. I have a tendency to talk to myself."

Luli smiled, "You didn't say nothin'," she said and reached forward to tap Avery's forehead with one perfect pink nail. "You didn't have to. Close your mouth, girl, or put a biscuit in it. You don't think you ended up here by accident, do you?"

Avery had read a good deal of Southern gothic novels as a girl and seen even more movies, and this was starting to take a decidedly Flannery O'Conner-ish turn. Luli turned her back to Avery and picked up a ladle. She poured a little gumbo into a tin cup, tasted it, and then reached for some spice. "Don't reckon you even noticed that little car of yours was stopped clean in the middle of a crossroads? 'Course you didn't and even if you had, you wouldn't have thought anything of it. Folks can't read a sign anymore. Not even when it latches onto them like a crawdad. "

"I want to make you a deal," Luli said. "And a crossroads is always the best place for it. There's not even a trick to it— for you at least. I want you to write a story about this place."

"I would," Avery said. "I mean, I was going to."

"I know," Luli said, "I knew that you were from the first time that you bit into that biscuit. But I need you to understand as well as write. I'm not sure why, except, well, maybe I'm lonely and more than a little tired. Maybe I don't just want an article. Maybe what I really want is a partner."

"A partner?" Avery said, surprised. "Why, I don't know anything about running a restaurant. I'm flattered, of course, but I never thought..."

Luli laughed. "That's not true, girl, and you know it. It's all you think about in your secret heart when you're alone, when you're in your dreams. You dream about tea cakes and wooden rolling pins and the scent of home. No one runs away so hard unless they're afraid, and folks fear their hope and dreams as much as any demon."

"Hopes. Dreams. Desire. That's what I know best in this big old world. Maybe they're the only things I've ever really known. Every man has a hole in him. A want at the center of his soul that he can't quite scratch. It's that want that keeps them coming back. And every time they do, I give them what they need and they give me the same. Until one day, they find that nothing on the menu quite satisfies them, that all their needs are meet and all their wants are gone."

"How is that possible?" Avery asked, "And even if it was, how could that be a bad thing—to have everything you want?"

Luli sighed and for a second she looked very old. Avery could see three faces flash before her—the girl, the cook, a woman impossibly ancient, older than the earth. Then Luli smiled and she was herself again, except for her eyes. "Only a child would say such a thing," she said, "Don't you know, girl, want is what the world runs on. It's what gets you up in the morning and keeps you going and what lays you down at night. Even your dreams are full up with hot, desperate need. The way I see it, folk aren't much more than their wants, and that's the way it's always been."

"What happens to them, then?" Avery asked. "The ones that don't want anymore, I mean."

Luli shrugged. "Don't know," she said, "They just go away. I reckon that they know there's nothing more we can do for each other." She looked out at the people seated on vinyl benches and at little linoleum tables. Not one of them looked up from his or her plate. Instead they focused on glasses of sweet tea, okra and turnip greens, barbecue and dumplings, and pieces of pie with meringue so fluffy and high that it looked like little clouds.

"I don't understand," Avery said, but she really did—or at least, thought she did. The biscuit had opened up a longing in her for home, but now it was gone. Was it because she was in some way home or because, well, Luli had eaten it?

"Every man's got to eat," Luli said, "even folk like me. We're all hungry in one way or t'other. In the old days, things were different. Cleaner. There was smoke and fire and offerings laid on altars covered in seashell and bone. Folks laid their hopes and dreams down and they got an answer—even if it was 'no.' But no one's straightforward these days. They're hungrier than ever, but they don't know what they want. In the old days, desire was ground cornmeal and plantains. That's how it is here, simple people, simple desires. You can go a long way with that. But a woman gets tired of the same old thing every day. I want desires like fine wines and overproofed rums. I want dreams as rich as jam cake and candied rose hips. What I want, need, is a desire that goes straight down to the soul. A need great enough to fill decades. Big city needs."

"It's a lot to take in, I know," Luli continued, "and it's not an offer I've made before. It's not even the offer I planned to make. You have a talent in you too, girl. Seems like you pulled the desire right out of me this time. But there it is. I want more than just this place. I want folks to say my name like they used to in the old days. I want them to come to me dripping with desire and to leave filled to the brim. I've let myself be satisfied with this little place, these little dreams. Me. The Queen of Desire bottled and stoppered like old vinegar. But I'm not vinegar, I'm a fine wine and I need space to breathe. You can help me with that, can't you, girl? And you want to do it, too."

Avery nodded. She noticed, for the first time, that the biscuit she'd been holding had crumbled to bits in her grasp. Around her, the kitchen steamed and she thought she could hear the roil of the ocean and the cries of strange birds. Were there drums? Maybe. Or maybe it was the beat of her heart. Luli walked over to the gumbo, dipped in the ladle twice, and returned with a steaming bowl so red it looked black. "Even gods don't live forever, girl," Luli said. "Well, they don't if they don't take care. You're an educated woman. I suppose you've read all those Greek legends about ambrosia, the food of the gods. But I don't suppose you ever thought the recipe for it would include okra and crayfish. Well, it takes more than molasses to make a good barbecue sauce and it takes more than ambrosia to make a god, but both are a good start."

Luli set the bowl down on the counter in front of Avery and walked back over to the oven. She took out two chess pies, cut them into pieces, and set them on the counter. When she looked back at Avery, the bowl was nearly empty. "It could do with some chili-infused mac and cheese, or maybe some coleslaw with honey jalapeno dressing as a side," Avery said. She held out the bowl and Luli dropped in another ladle's worth. The cook nodded and smiled.

Around the two women, pots boiled, tea brewed, and yeast bread rose. Out in the dining room, a man in a yellow jacket ordered two fried banana pies to go and a woman pushed away from another table satisfied. Avery and Erzulie sighed. It wasn't the ending to the day either of them had expected, but it was still a good one. Avery poured coffee into two white mugs while Erzulie dished up the pie still hot from the oven. Even when you're full, there's always a little room for dessert.

Chapter 38:
Wild Hearts

They say that wild hearts can't be tamed, but they can be broken.

Children don't have to be told things are magical. They believe in faeries, unicorns, and wishing wells by instinct. They know that a crossroads is a place where dreams can come true or go terribly wrong, and they know that monsters under the bed are all too real, and that they aren't just under the bed, but also in the closet and deep in the cellar. Monsters are everywhere. Children are afraid of things that go bump in the night because it's only good sense to be afraid. It's the adults that lock the windows, buy floodlights, and purchase alarm systems. It's the adults that try to confine the world to daylight and night. Every child knows there's as much menace in the shadows at the height of day as there is at midnight and that evil can lurk behind a pretty face and a bright smile.

Life and death, good and evil, truth and lies. A child knows them all with a look. Ghosts aren't frightening to children—they're a source of curiosity. Children aren't afraid of much until we teach them to be. And we often teach them to fear the wrong things.

When I was a little girl, I believed a unicorn lived in Ivy Hollow. The wood was green year-round, even when the rest of the wood was covered in snow. Someone older would've said that a hot spring ran under the place and someone younger mightn't have wondered at all. But I was the perfect age to believe in magic and every little girl wants to believe in unicorns. There are enough bad things in the world. So, by rights, there should be more than enough bright things to even the balance. Every child believes in puddles that open into bottomless wells and knows that the old darkness waits and watches from every dark corner and from under every bed. But they also know that there are places of light, sacred places, where an untamable wildness still runs free.

The problem is, of course, that trees don't get much of a say in things these days. Trees, stones, rivers, and the life that surrounds them all have a price tag on them. They can be bought and sold and traded—at least in theory. Whether the old spirits of the land agree is another matter. Maybe they don't care as long as things don't change too much. Age tends to lock a fellow into a certain way of thinking. And though the adage goes that age mellows a man, it tends to refine him, to pare him down to a few strong traits. If that's true of a person who lives three score and ten, then you can only imagine how much truer it would be of a river or a stone or the land itself. There's a good deal of people who'd say that only men have souls, but since there's no proof to be had to the contrary or the affirmative, a wise man would ere on the side of caution. But most men are not wise.

These are hard times and a man with land always has decisions to make. Whether land is in furrow or fallow, the taxes still come due. Corn and tobacco don't bring what they once did and a few cows are almost no better than none at all. Small farms have always had a hard row to hoe, literally and figuratively. Farmers know that sometimes you have to make hard choices if you want to keep land together, and one commodity that always draws an interest is trees.

Not just any trees, of course, but old-growth timber, those ancient oak, maple, and pine sentinels that you see along the highways and byways of the South. They cluster in groves in old knotted woods and hardwood forests in the borderlands and bayous, and down to the hard scrub land you hit along the Panhandle. A beech can have a life longer than a man's—but not much longer. Like many a man they falter and hollow and fall to rot in their old age. But an oak or a pine can reach a grand old age reaching up out of the canopy and heaping on

215

rings until it's too large for four grown men to circle with arms outstretched. These are the trees that fuel lumberyards and sawmills. As long as there are men, they will need houses and buildings and tables and chairs, and trees are the ones who pay the price for those needs.

When a crew decides to harvest some land, they survey the trees like plump turkeys before Thanksgiving, marking the ones meant to be harvested, others that need to be removed so their trucks and sledges can move the harvest away, and still others that are likely to fall and present a hazard to the men working the woods. Scrub trees like ironwood and sycamore tend to get rooted up or pushed over, big hollowed beeches are left unless they're likely to fall, and other trees are marked in red or yellow paint to indicate their status. Of course, the trees have their own hierarchy whether men recognize it or not and although animals can flee a lumber crew, the trees stay put.

There was an old oak tree that was reckoned to be the oldest in the county. Not so ancient as the Angel Oak, but still a tree of formidable age. It was a knotted thing, twisted at its height and the father of countless smaller oaks that lay in its shade. The lumber crew marked it in red, a great find that could be hewn and stripped and then hauled down to the pasture, placed on a logging truck once its height had been reduced to manageable chunks. Altogether, the King Oak and the trees around it were well worth the effort it would take to create logging roads, fell smaller trees, and drag them into the light. It was a good plan, well-laid, and following a hundred other plans the crew and their chief had made before, but for some reason, it didn't work.

The day the crew began work in the woods a low rain began to fall that lasted two weeks straight. A deep sucking mud made it impossible for the heavy trucks to move and landslides in the forest made even removing the smallest trees dangerous. After a month's delay, the crew began work only to find machinery inexplicably rusted, chains popped, and engines blown. The logging road took a month instead of a week to lay, and the smaller trees and scrub brush which usually took no more than a week or two to remove was subject to breaks, falls, and even a lightning strike that happened at the height of day with not a cloud in sight. The fire that broke out took the crew the rest of the day to quell and cost them a truck and two crew members who had to be taken to the hospital due to smoke inhalation. As the crew slogged through the woods, harassed by hornets, bats that flew out of hollow beeches, and even a rabid fox, the King Oak loomed above the forest like a ranger in his tower. But every day the crew inched a bit closer.

On the third month of cutting, a loaded truck rolled silently down the hillside, tipping and scattering its haul, as well as crushing the side of the vehicle. The following week, another rain began that eroded the logging road and washed gravel into the scree and rotted leaves that the crew stumbled over and found wedged into their boots for days. On the next week a loaded truck took two flat tires on the hillside and had to be unloaded for a tire change, losing the crew a day and causing the men to mutter to themselves about curses and spells and the anger of trees.

Throughout the weeks, the crew was plagued with allergies and colds, bug bites and stings, and even a case of boils. The crew chief was not a religious man, but he caught himself praying more than once and always his eyes were drawn to the King Tree in the distance. He found that there were mornings he remembered it in his dreams and it seemed to him that the tree watched him as diligently as he watched it.

Five months passed and the job was not half done, though the summer was in its final days. There were heaps of scrub trees piled in the pastures and fired nightly. Those fires lit the sky and spit embers that looked like thousand fireflies. Some of the crew members said the place must be cursed. They whispered it on their lunch breaks taken not in the shade of the woods, but in the safety of the hot, flat pasture. The eyed the

217

King Tree and muttered against it as their Chief took his lunch in his truck cab with the air conditioning set to high. There was a bitterness in the air, a high green smell that reminded them of unripe pecans crushed or wet baled hay. They pushed hard at their work and did not let the shadow of the King Oak fall on them.

Finally, after months of blood, sweat, and swearing, they reached the oak grove where the King Oak and his children stood and began the harvest. So long and bitter had been their march, that the crew chief demanded to strike and make the first cut himself. It had been years since he'd felled a tree, but symbolism has a deep impact on the superstitious. His men's muttering that morning had been so fierce, that he had a mind to put an end to it with one blow. It was cold in the grove. The King Oak and the other trees surrounding it had a tight canopy and only moss and dead leaves littered the ground. Men telling the story later would say that it was silent as well, an impossible thing in the woods at midday. The chief lifted the humming chainsaw and touched the tree and the impossible happened.

The tree that had been sounded and marked, cracked and shuddered and fell slowly forward. The Chief stumbled and skidded out of its way, but not fast enough. The tree closed around him, its great hollow center covering him like a canoe. He howled and beat the sides of the tree and with much care, his crew extricated him. They left that day, the King Oak felled and laying empty in the grove, the smaller oaks surrounding the ruin of their king.

That night, they burned the last of the scree and scrub, took assessment of their losses and carried the final harvested trees away. The King Oak no longer loomed above the canopy, but it was still there. And the next spring a fine scattering of tiny live oaks sprung up around the husk of the old tree. Some of those trees are now tall, though not as tall as their brothers, and none as mighty as the King Oak. From the King Oak's grove, you can see the logging roads and the furrows that the great trucks made up and down the hillside. But each season the marks are fainter, the road a little less defined, and the oaks a bit taller. The woods are forgetting, but the King Oak and his grove remember. They watch and they wait and they grow.

Chapter 39:
Flyaway Home

If this story wasn't true, it would end differently... some stories are almost too sad to tell.

Sorrow leaves its mark as clear as any wound. But, unlike a wound, it doesn't heal. It lays heavy in the fog on a winter's morning. It becomes a part of every breath taken, and though it doesn't stop a soul from breathing, it makes each day a labor. Places can have broken hearts, too. You find them all the time—fields and farms where even the stones seem to weep, places where a sadness too deep for men to bear crept into the very soil and colored the earth red. Carter House is such a place. You can feel a great sense of loneliness when you visit, a sense not of despair, but of hope held and lost. It's a place of unfinished business.

The Battle of Franklin was not a great battle by military standards. But it was unusual in more than a few ways. The band continued to play throughout the battle, much like those plucky souls who carried on even as the Titanic sank to its fate. It was a battle fought as much in dark as in light—a rarity during the Civil War, and it saw the end of six generals. The battle ranged throughout the town and these days many of the sites are covered by storefronts and golf courses. General Cleburne fell over by where a pizza place stood for many years. Carnton House and its gardens still stand. But much of its fields are now a golf course and houses. And Carter House is surrounded by beauty parlors, restaurants, and automotive stores. The house itself and a few of its outbuildings were saved only by Franklin's bustling tourist trade and the endeavors of local historic societies.

Unlike Carnton, Carter was never a great house. It was a fine house in its day, but a merchant's house nonetheless. The family who owned held less than three hundred acres of farmland and ran a thriving business cotton mill. The house and its outbuildings were considered fine, but not lavish and the Carters who lived in them were well-respected. Fountain Branch Carter was a widower, who had seen the death of his wife, Mary and four of his twelve children. His youngest son, Theodrick, lovingly known as Tod had been captured at Missionary Ridge. He managed to escape, jumping from a transit train while he and some other prisoners were being moved east, and was able to return to his regiment outside of Dalton, Georgia.

General John B. Hood's troops, to which Tod was attached, had faced General John M. Schofield two days before outside Spring Hill. Though Hood had lost half his strength in the Atlanta campaign, he hoped by cutting through the Carolinas and Tennessee he could stop Sherman's supply route, forcing him to turn from his March to the Sea. Hood's army outnumbered Schofield nearly two to one and Hood planned to hit them hard, but awoke the morning of November 30 to find Schofield and his 24,000 had marched passed the sleeping Confederate army in the night and into Franklin. Union troops woke the Carter family before dawn, requisitioning the house and grounds, and began laying siegeworks.

After nearly four years away from home, Tod found himself within miles of home, but unable to visit. Tod cut through the woods with plans to make his way to the Carter home, but found the Carter House already serving as headquarters for General Jacob D. Cox. The yard and Carter Hill were covered with Union troops who were tearing down the barns and family cotton mill to use as emplacements. A family friend spotted Tod and waved him off, so he turned his horse, Rosencrantz, and made his way back to the 20th Tennessee Infantry. Tod, now a captain, served as aide to General Thomas Benton Smith. In the past three and a half years he had fought at the battles of Mill Spring, Shiloh, Perryville, Murfreesboro, Chickmauga, Missionary Ridge, and the Atlanta campaign. He had been captured, imprisoned and escaped, and had written more than a few articles for Southern newspapers using the pen name, Mint Julep. On the morning of November 30, 1864, Tod Carter was twenty-four years old.

Despite their dug-in position, Hood ordered his generals to make a full frontal assault on the breastworks. Hood had lost his arm and leg and took laudanum to numb his pain, but it did little to assuage his grief. He had lost friends, family, and reputation during the war. Schofield and his men had slipped past him in the night passing less than a mile from where his sentries stood. Whether it was the will of God or the Devil, Hood didn't know, but he meant to crush his enemy. The day before the battle, he had berated his commanders for their performance at Spring Hill. Honor and hubris kept them silent as Hood gave orders for the next day. As for himself, he had placed his headquarters in a manor home across from Winstead Hill. He would stay there throughout the battle. General Patrick Cleburne, on hearing the orders, remarked only that the enemy's defenses were "formidable." He later said to a fellow officer, "If we must die, then let us die like men." He would not survive the day.

Some might say that God and the angels stand on the side of right. But in most wars, God favors the side with the best artillery. The Battle of Franklin was no different. Around four in the afternoon, the battle started in earnest. It was nearly sunset and, other than Gettysburg, the battlefield was one of the most open fields that had been encountered, offering little cover than a few outbuildings. The Carter family, their neighbors, and servants huddled in the cellar of the wood and brick house while the battle raged overhead. Of the two dozen people waiting out the battle, nearly half were children. So fierce was the fighting that Union soldiers took refuge in the cellar with the family until Fountain Branch's insults drove them back into the battle. Upstairs, Union and Confederate soldiers crouched within spitting distance of each other unable to move due to the hail of bullets and artillery. Within the hour, Tod Carter would be mortally wounded. As he mounted his horse, he was reported to have said, "Follow me boys, I'm almost home." He was felled within five hundred yards of his house. Carter's father, three sisters and sister-in-law searched for him by lantern. They found him in the early morning and carried him to his sister Annie's room. He died on December 2, 1864.

The Union forces held. Hood lost a third of his remaining strength and, as a result of the battle, his command. He also lost eight generals; six were killed, one captured, and one wounded. Patrick Cleburne was found with a single shot through his head, missing his boots, with his face respectfully covered with his hat. He and the five other generals who lost their lives in the battle were laid on the porch of Carnton House. The cemetery outside the house was the final resting place for soldiers on both sides of the battle.

Carter House still stands today marred by bullet hollows and sorrow. Though Tod never woke after his wound, visitors have seen his spirit sitting on the side of his sister Annie's bed, walking the halls, and resting in the parlor. It seems in death he finally found his way home.

Chapter 40:
Perfect Circle

Stories are living things and each time you tell the same story, it become a little bit more real. It stretches and breathes and changes a bit with the telling. There are some stories that get stuck in your head. They itch and tickle and claw like mice in the attic. They nibble at the edges of your mind until you just have to write them down or whisper them over a campfire. That's why you hear the same stories over and over with different names and places. They're the stories that have lived since the beginning of time. We were born with them and they'll be here long after we're gone. The only way we lose them is when they step into the light and become things of flesh and blood. It doesn't happen often, but it happens sometimes. It happens enough to give the other stories hope and to start them twisting and whispering in our dreams so that you wake up in the middle of the night and make a few notes on a piece of paper. In the morning, maybe you're lost the thought, but it hasn't lost you. It will keep coming back like a piece of loose thread in a sweater until you finally snag it and pull it free.

But sometimes the process works in reverse and a real thing becomes a story. Maybe the story, over time, becomes more real than the actual man or woman. It becomes a legend. Legends are powerful things. Cities and countries and civilizations have been built around them. The fall of Troy gave birth to the legend of the founding of Rome. Whether it's true or not doesn't matter so long as people believe it's true. Belief is always stronger than fact. Fact is a solid enough thing, but belief can call things out of memories, it can create miracles, and it can stir dreams. At the core of every story is a crumb of hope that the story is true, or that perhaps it isn't.

There are some things that are too beautiful to exist outside of paper and ink and some things to terrible to breathe outside of the mind's eye. It's a wise man who knows the difference.

Take ghost stories for example. Almost every town has a haunted house. It has a swayed porch, a screen door that hangs askew and paint that hasn't seen a paint brush in a month of Sundays. There's usually a broken tire swing, a couple of gnarled old trees, and a rusty weathervane that catches the wind. There's a story about the house. Someone died there. No one can quite remember who, but if you knock on the door three times, or open the mail box, or say a name three times while looking in the mirror, the ghost will appear. You have to wonder after a while what came first—the ghost or the ghost story? Was the house really haunted or did all that belief call a ghost into existence? Maybe the spirit was a bit fuzzy around the edges, but it knew where it lived, and as the stories grew, it was given a name and a history and it came into being as surely as a story written on a page. After ten years or twenty everyone in town could tell you about the house and the ghost and maybe a few people even wrote the story down for posterity. Others told it around campfires and at sleepovers until the story became as clear as the inscription on a monument. Until the story was so real that it was as if it actually had happened. There isn't, after all, much difference between a legend and a memory.

There's a haunted house on our street. Everyone knows it's haunted, but no one says so. No one has lived in it for more than six months at a time. Dogs and cats shy away from it. Children hesitate when a ball rolls into its front lawn. And even the pizza delivery car refuses to turn around in its driveway. There's just something wrong with that house. Not that you could really say what it was. It looks perfectly respectable. The owner, who is desperate to rent it, keeps its walls painted, its yard neatly trimmed, and the mailbox surrounded by pansies and begonias. But there's an indefinable wrongness about it. It slants toward the street expectantly like it hopes to catch someone unaware in its shadow. And, then, there's the drip. There's always a slow trickle of water that flows from the houses yard and a slight smell of mold. It could all be easily explained by the angle of the street, a subterranean stream, or a dozen other perfectly natural things that might combine to give its white-washed walls a greenish patina and the air around it a tinge of cold. That is, of course, if you don't believe in ghosts.

But if you do believe in ghosts, then it's hard to believe that this particular house isn't haunted. It's just too off. It's the kind of place that, if you had to walk by it as a kid, you would've quickened your pace and averted your eyes—only to stare back at the last minute because the only thing worse than seeing is not seeing the thing creeping up behind you. The funny thing, though, is that no one has ever seen a ghost in this particular house. Children on the street draw pictures on the street in chalk of a house streaming round-mouthed white ghosts with an arrow pointing in its direction and the disclaimer: *This House is Haunted.* As you can imagine, that doesn't do a lot to encourage potential buyers or even renters—although it may attract occupants of a particular kind. After all, ghosts need a place to live. There are as many kinds of ghosts as there are of people. More, really, since there are ghosts of trees and battles and memories. Ghosts need a place to lay their figurative heads, and once a house is labeled as haunted it tends to become a haunted house in fact as much as in legend.

Over the years, we've seen renters come and go and now the house is empty. Or is it? Maybe it has new unseen occupants who don't mind the steady drip of water that flows around the yard, the green-paned windows, or the low smell of mold. If you close your eyes, you could almost imagine a river running through the place, which, I've been told there once was. It has long since dried up except, perhaps, in the land's memory. So, the house sits and waits and we watch it and perhaps it watches us as well. After all, it is a haunted house. Everyone says so.

CPSIA information can be obtained
at www.ICGtesting.com
Printed in the USA
LVHW080028210219
608273LV00030B/823/P